COMPOSERS' LETTERS

12. 1. 22

SAVOY HOTEL.
LONDON.
W.C.2.

Verehrter Freund!

Ich danke Ihnen herzlich für Ihren lieben Brief und den erneuten Ausdruck Ihrer mir stets so wertvollen Sympathie. Leider ist mein Sohn krank und ich kann in den nächsten Tagen nur schwer das Hotel verlassen. Seien Sie so freundlich, mir mitzuteilen, wann und wo ich Sie sehen kann. Mit besten Empfehlungen auch an Ihre Gemahlin Ihr

unverändert verehrungsvoll ergebener

Richard Strauss.

A letter from Richard Strauss to Edward Elgar, January 12, 1922.

COMPOSERS' LETTERS

Edited by

JAN FIELDEN

*M*arginalia
PRESS

First published in 1994 by
Marginalia Press,
an imprint of
Ippon Books Ltd
55 Long Lane,
London N3 2HY

ISBN (Hardback): 1 874572 75 5
ISBN (Paperback): 1 874572 85 2

Thanks: Roy Fielden, Heather Godwin, Adam Green, Perry Keenlyside, Nicolas Soames, and Gramophone for access to the library.

Origination and Reprographics by Ads, St Albans, Hertfordshire
Printed by Redwood Books, Trowbridge, Wiltshire

CONTENTS

INTRODUCTION

"But what need is there to go dragging letters out of a composer of music? Letters that are always written in haste, carelessly, as something of no importance, because a composer does not realise he is expected to uphold his reputation as a literary man. Isn't it enough that they hiss him for his notes? Not a bit of it! Letters as well! Ah, fame is a great nuisance! Poor little famous great men, they pay a high price for popularity! Never an hour's peace alive or dead. ..."

In this letter, written in 1882, Giuseppe Verdi expresses his doubts about the wisdom of publishing collections of composers' letters, in this case the 'poor little famous great' man was Vincenzo Bellini. However, it is to our advantage that composers over the centuries, have been prolific writers of letters to fellow musicians, patrons and publishers as well as to their families and friends. Many letters have survived to appear in published collections, both in their lifetimes and in the following centuries when the continuing popularity of their music gave them historic status.

In these letters, as well as in their music, we can hear the voices of the composers themselves. They are speaking directly, often frankly and with feeling. Through their own words expressed simply on paper and committed to the postal services – whatever they may have been like at the time – a portrait of the composer as a human being emerges. Frequently, this shows a different, perhaps unexpected side to the master of sound and artifice known through a series of symphonies or concertos.

It is impossible to give a rounded portrait of each composer through such a small selection of correspondence that a book of this size can contain. Instead, I have tried to bring alive the personality of each individual through one or two incidents or aspects of what has so often proved an eventful and complex life.

From the truly fascinating – and huge – library of letters that exists from European composers of the past four centuries, I have chosen several broad themes. These include creativity, the struggles of earning a living, friendships (particularly with other composers), romance, composers' place in society, travelling, and of course, performances.

The collection begins in the sixteenth century with Claudio Monteverdi and ends in the mid-twentieth, with Benjamin Britten. The letters have been chosen for their style and vivacity and their ability to throw light on a certain subject – hence a letter from the minor composer, Ivor Gurney, is deemed as worth including for its description of the first World War as are letters from Verdi describing his problems with the Neapolitan censors.

Over the centuries the status and role of the composer has changed. Monteverdi, Bach and Mozart were little more than servants or tradesmen to minor princes or city and church officials now long forgotten, except for their, often parsimonious, patronage of their "servants". Fortunately their creativity survived to leave us the *Vespers of 1610*, the *Mass in B Minor* and *Cosi fan Tutti!*

In the eighteenth century and before, composers were usually paid a pittance and there are many examples of letters to their patrons pleading for more money or for better conditions for their choirs or orchestras. In the case of Wolfgang Amadeus Mozart and his father, on the pay-roll of the Archbishop of Salzburg, we hear of Mozart's strenuous attempts to supplement his income by organizing concert-tours and teaching.

Gradually, as the centuries passed by, composers became less dependent and were able to live, though often precariously, from their earnings from their music, unincumbered by a commanding patron. As the practice of subscription concerts and private and public commissions developed so they became more independent.

It is striking, on reading the correspondence of composers, how organized they had to be – so often their own publicists, agents, travel managers. Nowadays the pressure is relieved by agents, though a well organized, worldly musician is still at an advantage.

The community of composers has always been important. Few people like working in a vacuum and it becomes evident through the letters how composers thrive on musical gossip, meeting and playing with other musicians, writing letters, listening to each other's work. This is all reflected in the following pages. The influence of one composer upon another is important. For example Frederick Delius, Edvard Grieg, and Ralph Vaughan Williams inspired each other and supported each other and it was Grieg's interest in folk music that set Percy Grainger off in this direction. And of course there are the jealousies. We read how Mozart couldn't abide Gluck, how Debussy, having flirted with Wagner, discarded him for his own, individual voice and how Prokofiev and Stravinsky had an uneasy, competitive relationship. The letters between Benjamin Britten, W.H. Auden and other contemporaries illustrate the eagle eye they each keep upon each other's creations.

Most of the composers in this book were also excellent teachers, probably because they had something of excellence to impart. Thus we read of Mozart's struggles to teach composition to a young girl in Paris, Britten's advice in a letter to a teenage composer and Monteverdi and Bach's painstaking attention to the welfare of their choirs.

Despite the gradual change in status of composers, there remains a constancy of themes in their letters. The struggle to get on and do what they wanted and not what was expedient, the struggle to make a living, the common experience of the hurt inflicted by the critics. (Elgar was particularly wounded in this way.)

Each composer experiences the events and turmoils of his age and this is reflected in music. Heinrich Schutz had to cope with the Thirty Years War, Lully and Gluck's music reflected the elegance of court life in Paris before the revolution and the Russian composers of the 1918 revolution speak through their music declaring their support for the people. Auden wrote in a letter to Britten, "If you are really to develop to your full stature, you will have, I think, to suffer, and make others suffer, in ways which are totally strange to you at present, and against every conscious value that you have; i.e. you will have to be able to say what you never yet have had the right to say – God, I'm a shit..."

In compiling this book I have been forcibly reminded that though music was the primary creative medium of these composers, they have proved to be expressive letter writers. I hope that, you too, in reading these letters, gain fresh insight into the lives and times of those who wrote the music that we so admire.

Jan Fielden

CLAUDIO MONTEVERDI
1567 – 1643

Monteverdi was born in the Italian town of Cremona and entered the service of the Duke of Mantua in 1602 as Director of Music. There he remained until the death of his patron in 1613. It was at the court of Mantua that his first important opera *Orpheus* received its premiere in 1607. He then became *maestro di cappella* at St Marco in Venice where he stayed until his death at seventy-six. Whilst at St Marco, Monteverdi remained close to the court at Mantua.

Monteverdi was one of the earliest composers to confront the complexities of combining the staging of opera with the particular demands of the libretti and his letters to the Duke regarding forthcoming opera productions show his strength of character and conviction. He was never afraid to stick by his principles when it came to his work even though he was the Duke's servant.

Although Monteverdi had a voice of his own he knew his place and when necessary could be self effacing, as in his letter to Cardinal Ferdinando Gonzaga at Rome:

MONTEVERDI TO CARDINAL FERDINANDO GONZAGA

I have just now received Your Eminence's very kind letter together with the two most beautiful madrigals set to music; and I read and re-read the letter, I at once sang the music to myself over and over, and kissed the one and the other again and again with extreme rejoicing, seeing in that letter how great Your Eminence's affection is towards one of his lowliest servants, as I am, who deserve nothing.

Monteverdi's salary hardly made up for his increasing responsibilities, and to make matters worse his wages were being paid late, as were those of his wife and her father, who were both court musicians. The cause was an unco-operative treasury official. Eventually, his patience exhausted, he was forced to appeal directly to the Duke. Nevertheless, throughout this difficult period he continued to write wonderful music: madrigals, church music, ballets and operas. Like Mozart, outside pressures seemed not to impair his creativity nor the quality of his work.

MONTEVERDI TO DUKE VINCENZO GONZAGA

Mantua, 27 October 1604;

Most Serene Lord, my Most Respected Master,

As final recourse it is indeed proper that I appeal to Your Highness's infinite virtue, since it is that which in the end directs your will concerning the salary granted to me by your kindness. I therefore kneel before you with the greatest possible humility, and beg you to be so good as to cast your gaze not upon boldness (perhaps) in writing this letter, but rather upon my great distress, which is the reason for my writing; not upon the Lord President, who on numerous occasions has given an affirmative order so very kindly and politely, but rather upon Belintento, who never wanted to carry it out except when it pleased, and now that it has come down to this, I have almost had to accustom myself to being beholden to him – and not to the infinite virtue of Your Highness, who through his boundless good will grant favours even to servants of little merit such as I am compared with the widespread regard for Your Highness's great merit – although behaving in a most unmannerly way towards me when he did not want to give me such payments.

This humble petition of mine comes to you with no other aim but to beg Your Highness kindly to direct that I receive wages amounting to a total of five months, in which situation my wife Claudia and my father-in-law also find themselves, and this sum grows even larger since we do not see any hope of being able to get hold of future payments save by the express command of Your Highness, without which support all that I have been building up will be ruined and undone, since misfortunes continue to overwhelm me day in and day out, and I have not the means to remedy them.

Nevertheless, to obtain these payments (at least of one month only, if not all) I have used nothing but prayers, humility, and politeness morning and night, by virtue of which exertion I have lost and am still losing practically all the time for study that I ought to devote to the taste and requirements of Your Highness, finding myself as I do in a reasonable position and favoured by you, and yet I can obtain nothing.

If I am worthy to receive it of Your Highness's infinite virtue, I beg you from the bottom of my heart to grant me this particular favour, which is not only that I be paid, but (and this I shall feel each time as an even greater favour) that I not be paid by the hand of Belintento, for I am sure that Your Highness could find someone other than him who would give me some satisfaction, at least in words if not in deeds, at least in honour if not in results, at least once if not every time. Nor do I know why this man goes on behaving thus towards me.

If this favour of yours were to extend over the customs duties of Viadana, we would be entirely satisfied; and I thus assured by Your Highness's infinite virtue and by the many other outstanding graces and kindnesses granted to me, hope also to be favoured (by virtue of such graces and kindnesses) with that which I have requested of Your Highness. Being capable of no more, I shall pray that Our Lord grant a long life to Your Highness, to whom I bow and make a most humble reverence.

from Mantua, 27 October 1604
Your Most Serene Highness's
most humble and most grateful servant
Claudio Monteverdi

In 1607 Monteverdi took his sick wife and their son back to Cremona. When his wife died his health broke down and, overcome with grief and exhaustion from overwork, he requested honourable dismissal from his position at court. The release he so much desired was not granted for over three years.

MONTEVERDI TO ANNIBALE CHIEPPIO, (COUNCILLOR)

Cremona,
2 December 1608

Today, which is the last day of November, I received from Your Lordship a letter from which I learned of His Highness's command: that I come as soon as possible to Mantua. Most Illustrious Signor Chieppio, if he orders me to come and wear myself out again, I assure you that unless I take a rest from toiling away at music for the theatre, my life will indeed be a short one, for as a result of my labours (so recent and of such magnitude) I have had a frightful pain in my head and so terrible and violent an itching around my waist, that neither by cauteries which I have applied to myself, nor by purges taken orally, nor by blood-letting and other potent remedies has it thus far been possible to get better – only partly so. My father attributes the cause of the headache to

3

mental strain and the itching to Mantua's air (which does not agree with me), and he fears that the air alone could be the death of me before long. Just think then, Your Lordship, what the addition of brainwork would do....

Dear Sir, help me to obtain an honourable dismissal, for it seems to me that it is the best possible thing, because I shall have a change of air, work and fortune; and who knows, if the worst comes to the worst what else can I do but to remain poor as I am? As regards my coming to Mantua to secure my dismissal with His Highness's kind approval, unless he wish it otherwise this much will I do, assuring Your Lordship that I shall always proclaim His Highness as my lord and master, wherever I am, and shall always acknowledge him with my humble prayers to Almighty God; more than this I cannot do.

MONTEVERDI TO ANNIBALE IBERTI (COURT OFFICIAL, AT MANTUA).

Venice,
21 November, 1615

His Highness of Mantua's Most Illustrious Resident dwelling in Venice, very much my master, commissioned me recently through Your Lordship's letter (at the command of His Highness of Mantua, my particular Lord) to set a ballet to music; but the commission did not go into any other detail, unlike those of the Most Serene Lord Duke Vincenzo – may he be in glory! – who used to demand of me such productions either in six, eight or nine movements, besides which he used to give me some account of the plot, and I used to try and fit to it the most apt and suitable music, and the metrical schemes that I knew.

However, believing that a ballet of six movements should turn out to be to His Highness's liking, I straight away tried to finish the enclosed, of which two movements were lacking; and this in fact I began in recent months in order to present it to His Highness, thinking that I would be in Mantua this past summer for certain business affairs of mine.

While I am sending it off by the hand of the Resident to Your Lordship, to present to His Highness, I also thought it a good idea to accompany it with a letter of mine addressed to Your Lordship, to tell you at the same time that if His Highness should want either a change of tune in this ballet, or additions to the enclosed movements of a slow or grave nature, or fuller and without imitative passages (His Highness taking no notice of the present words which can easily be changed, though at least these words help by the nature of their metre and by imitating the melody), or if he should want everything altered I beg you to act on my behalf so that His Highness may be so kind as to reword the commission, since as a most devoted servant, and most desirous of acquiring His Highness's favour, I shall not fail to carry it out in such a way that His Highness will be satisfied with me.

But if by good fortune the enclosed should be to his liking, I would think it proper to perform it in a half-moon, at whose corners should be placed an arch lute and a harpsichord, one each side, one playing the bass for Chloris and the other for Thyris, each of them holding a lute, and playing and singing themselves to their own instruments and to the aforementioned. If there could be a harp instead of a lute for Chloris that would be even better.

Then having reached the ballet movement after they have sung a dialogue, there could be added to the ballet six more voices in order to make eight voices in all, eight *viole da braccio*, a contrabass, a *spinet arpata*, and if there were also two lutes, that would be fine. And directed with a beat suitable to the character of the melodies, avoiding over-excitement among the singers and players, and with the understanding of the ballet-master, I hope that – sung in this way – it will not displease His Highness.

Also, if you could let the singers and players see it for an hour before His Highness hears it, it would be a very good thing indeed. It has been unusually precious to me, this present opportunity, not so much for showing myself very prompt in obeying His Highness's commands, which I so much desire and long for, as to commend myself to Your Lordship as a loyal servant, praying that you may wish to maintain me, and condescend to command me.

Alessando Striggio, yet another court official, had already supplied Monteverdi with the libretto for *Orfeo* in 1607. He was to become his special ally and protector.

Venice,
9 February 1619

MONTEVERDI TO ALESSANDRO STRIGGIO (AT MANTUA)

I have received your Lordship's previous letter and the present one, but with this delay, however, because I went with my elder son Francesco to

Bologna (as the first feast-days of Christmas were over) and had the chance to remove him from Padua – to remove him from the splendid time which the Most Illustrious Lord Abbot Morosini* was kindly giving him so as to enjoy a little of the boy's singing. And in the long run he would have turned out to be a good singer with all the other additions (as one would say – though it is better to keep quiet about that), rather than an average doctor; and yet my way of thinking would prefer him to be good in the second profession and mediocre in the first, as if it were an ornament.

So, for the sake of helping the boy (as indeed I have done) and for my own satisfaction, I went – as I said – to settle him in Bologna as a boarder with the Servite fathers, in which priory they read and debate every day. And I was there for this purpose for about fifteen days, so that what with going and coming back and stopping there, I can say that I had hardly reached Venice when Your Lordship's aforementioned first letter was handed over to me.

And even if I had not received this second one from the post a moment ago – as the debtor I was as regards replying to Your Lordship's most kind letter – I had determined to let Your Lordship know (by the courier who is returning) just what I have told you above in this letter. I hope that, as a very kind person, you will accept this my true excuse as legitimate; and I do assure you that if I had received the first letter in time, and had not been hindered by an urgent duty, I would already have carried into effect what you were kind enough to command me.

But since Your Lordship is pleased to have the ballet for this Easter, you may be sure of receiving it, for I would not tolerate so great a deficiency in myself (in not doing all I can to serve you) if I wanted to maintain myself, through results, as much your servant as I profess to be, both in speech and in writing.

> The perils of travelling in the early seventeeth century are vividly described in the next letter.

MONTEVERDI TO ANNIBALE IBERTI

Venice,
12 October 1613

I am writing to let Your Lordship know how, being in the company of the Mantuan courier and leaving with him for Venice, we were robbed at Sanguinetto (not the actual place, but rather two miles away from it) by three

Monsignor Giovanni Francesco Morosini, Abbot of Leno and Canon of Padua.

ruffians –bandits – in this manner. Suddenly from a field adjoining the main road there came two men of brownish complexion, not much beard, and of medium height, with a musket apiece (the flint-wheel type) and the firing pin down. Then, one of these approaching on my side to frighten me with the musket, and the other holding on to the bridle of the horses – which went along quietly – they drew us aside into that field without saying a word.

And making me kneel down as soon as I had dismounted, one of the two who had the muskets demanded my purse, and the other demanded the cases from the courier. They were pulled down from the carriage by the courier, who opened them for him one by one, that assassin taking what he liked, and having everything given to him promptly by the courier. I was still on my knees all the while, guarded by the other one who had a gun, and in this manner they took whatever they wanted, as the third of the three assassins, who had a spike in his hand and had acted as lookout, was continuing to do this, making sure that nobody should enter from the road.

When they had well and truly turned over all the goods, the one who was looking into the things obtained from the courier came up to me and told me to undress myself because he wanted to see whether I had any other money. Having made sure that I did not, he went over to my maidservant for the same purpose, but she – helping her cause with all manner of prayers, entreaties and lamentations – made him leave her alone. Then, turning to the things and cases, he made a bundle of the best and finest, and while looking for something to cover himself with found my cloak – a long one of serge, brand new – which I had just had made for me in Cremona.

He said to the courier, 'Put this cloak on me': but when the assassin saw that it was too long for him, he said: 'Give me another one.' So he took my son's, but finding it too short, the courier then said, 'Look master, it belongs to that poor seminarian – give it to him;' and he complied. The courier also found the said boy's suit and did the same, and then when he asked with many entreaties for the maidservant's things as a gift, the ruffian handed them over to him. They made a huge bundle of the remainder, took it on their shoulders, and carried it away. Then we picked up the things that were left and went off to the inn ...

When I was in Mantua, I enjoyed the favour from the Lord President of having six months' salary, and I am also due for another, due three months ago. I told him of my great misfortune. If you were to try and put in a good

7

word for me with the Lord President (although I know that the Lord President's kindness is great) I would regard it as the greatest favour because, Sir, I have infinite need of it.

As with many commissioned works, time is the enemy:

MONTEVERDI TO ALESSANDRO STRIGGIO

Venice
9 January 1620

I am sending Your Lordship the lament of Apollo. By the next post I shall send you the beginning, up to this point, since it is already almost finished; a little revision in passing still remains to be done. At the place where Amore begins to sing, I would think it a good idea if Your Lordship were to add three more short verses of like metre and similar sentiment, so that the same tune could be repeated (hoping that this touch of gladness will not produce a bad effect when it follows – by way of contrast – Apollo's previous doleful mood), and then go on as it stands, changing the manner of expression in the music, just as the text does.

I would have sent Your Lordship this song by the last post, but Signor Marigliani (in a letter addressed to me) has passed a formidable request from Signor Don Vincenzo: that I finish the *Andromeda* – already begun – a fable by the aforementioned Signor Marigliani, so that it can be performed for His Highness this carnival time, on his return from Casale. But just as I am having to do a bad job through being obliged to finish it in a hurry, so too I am thinking that it will be badly performed and badly played because of the acute shortage of time. I am also greatly surprised that Signor Marigliani wishes to involve himself in such a dubious enterprise, since even if it had been begun before Christmas, there would hardly be time to rehearse it, let alone learn it.

Now consider, Your Lordship: what do you think can be done when more than 400 lines, which have to be set to music, are still lacking? I can envisage no other result than bad singing of the poetry, bad playing of the instruments, and bad musical ensemble. These are not things to be done hastily, as it were; and you know from *Arianna* that after it was finished and learned by heart, five months of strenuous rehearsal took place.

Therefore if I could be certain that, through Your Lordship's influence, the

Prince's choice might fall upon Your Lordship's ballet (assuming however that this meets with your approval) I would expect this to be sufficient and would really succeed because I would have just enough time for such a short work. Then at my convenience, I could finish off the *Andromeda*, and you could have it learned in ample time (afterwards letting it be heard to good effect) so that I could attend with more care and thought to that ballet of yours that I am talking about.

Otherwise, being obliged to serve Signor Don Vincenzo and Your Lordship in so little time, I continue to think that the music I send will certainly be unsuitable rather than suitable; and I know you will admit that I am right, because you will take into account the fact that my ecclesiastical service has somewhat alienated me from the musical style of the theatre, and so before the style has become familiar again (what with the shortage of time and the need to write much) I shall have to send mere notes rather than something appropriate ...

Monteverdi was a very caring father. As he mentioned in one of the previous letters he was still keen for his son to become a doctor. Here we read of his attempt to raise the funds.

MONTEVERDI TO CATERINA MEDICI GONZAGA, DUCHESS OF MANTUA

Venice,
7 August 1621

Most Serene Lady, I have a son aged sixteen-and-a-half years – a subject and most humble servant of Your Highness – who has now left the seminary at Bologna, having completed there the course in humanistic studies and rhetoric. I would like him to go on to the other sciences in order to obtain a doctorate in medicine. He has always been under the discipline of tutors who have kept him in the fear of God and on the right lines of study.

Considering his liveliness and the licentious freedom of students (because of which fact they fall oftentimes into bad company, which diverts them from the rightful path, causing sorrow to their fathers and a tremendous loss to themselves), and in order to ward off the great harm that could come about, I thought that a place in the college of the Most Illustrious Lord Cardinal Mont'Alto – which he has in Bologna – would be a real boon to me, and the salvation of my son; but without a royal hand to aid me in so great a need it would not be possible for me to obtain such an outstanding favour.

Knowing therefore that Your Highness is by nature a princess full of infinite kindness towards everyone, in particular towards her respectful subjects, as is this poor boy, and to servants (though lowly) like myself, I have on this account been so bold as to beg Your Highness with most heartfelt sincerity (as I am doing) and with the most humble respect of which I am capable, that you may be so kind as to write in recommendation of such a place for the aforementioned son in the aforesaid college in Bologna to the Cardinal Mont'Alto, so that he may receive so lofty a favour.

But if at present all the places are filled, the first vacancy would still be in time.

MONTEVERDI TO ALESSANDRO STRIGGIO

Venice,
18 September 1627

I received at Parma two of Your Lordship's letters: on the one you instructed me to let you have *Armida*, which was much to the liking of the Most Serene Lord Duke my master, and likewise that I should come to Mantua; and in the other Your Lordship instructed me to busy myself getting hold of a male soprano of the best quality. I answered neither the one nor the other because I was doing my best, day after day, to return to Venice and serve you from there.

On my return to Venice three days ago, I at once handed over *Armida* for recopying: I shall be sending this to your Lordship by the next post, and informing you about the castrato, for in Parma the best is said to be Signor Gregorio, who is in the service of His Eminence Cardinal Borghese, but could (with considerable effort) get away, I should think. There is also Signor Antonio Grimano, but you could hardly hope to engage him. There are two others who have also come from Rome: some castrato who sings in St. Peter's, but he seems not very good to me because he has a voice that suffers from catarrh – not too clear, stiff ornaments, and very little *trillo*, then there is a boy of about eleven, but he seems not to have a pleasing voice either – he can do little ornaments and something of a *trillo*, but everything is pronounced with a somewhat muffled voice.

Regarding these two, I shall put out a feeler if Your Lordship wishes, but concerning the others I think I would not do anything. Nevertheless I have let them know about it, and since I am returning (if it please God) on the 2nd or 3rd of next month, I shall be better able to inform Your Lordship, as I have been late in receiving Your Lordship's very kind letters.

About my coming to Mantua, I shall also have to be excused at present, for because of my reputation I am not allowed to go there since my son Massimiliano is in the prisons of the Holy Office. He has been there for three months, the reason being that he read a book which he did not know was prohibited. He was accused by the owner of the book, who got himself imprisoned, and was deceived by the owner who said that the book dealt only with medicine and astrology. As soon as Massimiliano was in prison, the Father Inquisitor wrote to me saying that if I gave him a pledge of 100 ducats for being legally represented until the case was dispatched, he would release him at once.

In one of his letters, Signor Ercole Marigliani, the councillor, offered of his own accord to protect my son, and because of this known partiality of his, I begged him to pass on the task of arranging for my security payment to the Father Inquisitor to come out of the annual income paid to me by that Most Serene Prince my master, but since two months have gone by without my receiving an answer either from the Father Inquisitor or from Signor Marigliani, I am turning (with the greatest possible reverence) to Your Lordship's protection in delegating this particular matter to Signor Marigliani, in Massimiliano's favour and in accordance with his interests.

If he does not wish to undertake this security settlement, I shall always be ready to deposit 100 ducats so that my son can be released. I would indeed have done this already had I received a reply from Signor Marigliani. While Your Lordship will be helping my son (and of this I am most certain), I shall pray Our Lord for your well-being on this most holy feast of Christmas, and for a happy new year.

HEINRICH SCHÜTZ
1585 – 1672

Schutz was born in the German province of Thuringia exactly one hundred years before Bach and his music bridges the gap between the music of Palestrina and Byrd and that of Bach and Handel. As a boy he was a chorister in the choir of the court chapel in Cassel. From 1609 to 1612 he was a pupil of Giovanni Gabrieli in Venice where Gabrieli was organist at San Marco. It seems likely that during this time Schutz would have met Monteverdi. He returned to Cassel as church organist before entering the life-time service of the Elector of Saxony as Master of Music in Dresden in 1615. Schutz did however keep in touch with musical developments in Italy by means of frequent visits.

His life was beset by personal upheavals, and by the disruption of the Thirty Years War (1618 – 1648) which devastated agriculture, trade and everyday life in Germany.

His letters reveal some of the problems that beset him as Master of Music and of his concern for his players as he tried to get money for them and even strings for their instruments.

Schutz died virtually unrecognised but his music heralded that of Bach who was born thirteen years later.

SCHÜTZ TO KAMMERSEKRETAR LUDWIG MOSER

Dresden

3 July 1621

...As matters stand, I can not forbear to importune my most gracious Master with this present letter, it being my duty to report that not long since a sum of money was sent to Nuremberg from the Elector's exchequer here, wherewith to purchase strings for the Elector's orchestra from a wire-drawer of that place, by name Jobst Meuler, who manufactures steel strings for instruments, of such excellence that their like is impossible to be found elsewhere.

Now the aforesaid wire-drawer has indeed assured me in writing that he has the best will to give us satisfaction and prepare the strings; but that his fellow craftsmen will not give him leave to make anything out of the ordinary and better than they can do. Unless perchance a little order might be sent from our most gracious Master to the Town Council of Nuremberg, in which case he would surely be permitted.

Since, therefore, most gracious Herr Kammersekretar, I and my fellows in our profession set no less store by good strings than does a soldier, for example, by a pair of good pistols or other weapons, I trust you will not take it amiss that I trouble you in the matter.

And I hereby most humbly beg that without hesitation you obtain such a little order from our most gracious Master to the Nuremberg Council regarding the aforesaid Jobst Meuler, that he shall prepare the best strings for the Electoral Court in such quantity as may be ordered, and send it to me on the earliest occasion (by reason that a few days hence a messenger who understands these matters is to leave here for that place).

This is not only for the benefit of the whole orchestra but also to the advantage of our most gracious Elector and master, inasmuch as he will receive good wares for the money...

> With the war dragging on, Schütz applied again for leave of absence to make a journey to Copenhagen, where he had found a well-disposed patron in a prince of the Royal family, who later became the son-in-law of the Elector of Saxony. The following application was granted.

Dresden
9 February 1633

Most Humble Petition to his Serene Highness the Elector of Saxony and my Most Gracious Lord

...First to beg Your Serene Highness with my most humble devotion... graciously to permit me in the approaching Springtime to make the journey to Northern Germany for which I have several times humbly sought opportunity, to which end I would once again, in all obedience, bring to the notice of Your Serene Highness:

That while awaiting the outcome of the present ebb and flow of war I could well absent myself, since amid these events there is little need to set up an extensive ensemble; the company for players and singers is moreover somewhat weakened and reduced, some of them, owing to age and infirmity, being no longer able to appear, and others having departed to the war or on their own affairs, so that it would in any case be impossible to bring together a large orchestra or chorus.

That the orchestra is organized while I remain here (and which – according to present circumstances – may perhaps still suffice and be good) would nevertheless remain at your disposal and would not decline owing to my absence; likewise before my departure, with the knowledge of our Inspector, it would be put into good order and so left.

Also, that this my absence for a time would be a convenient means and good preparation for the future reformation and betterment of our *Collegii* (if the times will but permit of such a thing once more).

That the purpose of this my journey is again solely to escape for a while from the difficulties and impediments occasioned in our beloved fatherland by war and other circumstances, by which I too am affected, and in some place in Northern Germany to pursue my profession zealously and without disturbance of mind.

Moreover, in loyal obedience I cannot conceal from Your Serene Highness that a short while since, with no thought or striving on my part, the young elected royal Prince of Denmark enquired of me through Friedrich Lebseltern (Agent of the Elector's Court) whether with your most gracious leave I could visit him for the better reformation and arrangement of his music, he assuring that he would remember it in my favour and would release me again whenever desired.

Now not only would this perhaps give pleasure to that renowned royal Prince, the beloved future son-in-law of our most gracious Lord, while to me such attendance upon him would likewise be something useful and profitable; but my absence for so short a time would be of no harm whatsoever to the Elector's music.

I therefore beg, and hope the more, that your Serene Highness may graciously receive this, my most submissive and perhaps not immodest petition...

Between 1633 and 1645 Schütz made three visits to Copenhagen, where he organized the Court Chapel. In Dresden he tried persistently to save at least some remnants of his once numerous and excellent ensemble.

SCHÜTZ TO THE ELECTOR OF SAXONY

Dresden,
7 March 1641

...Although at the present time my most humble reminder (with respect to our now almost completely ruined orchestra) might, in view of the continued sad circumstances of our beloved fatherland, be regarded as untimely, even perhaps by Your Serene Highness, yet I hope to escape the reproach of unreasonableness and win your most gracious pardon; for even as the physician is in duty bound to tend a dangerous sickness before it takes a fatal turn, so must I succour our Corpus Musicum which now lies, as it were, at the last gasp...

But Your Serene Highness, being of a lofty understanding, is well able to judge and determine unaided when and how far (the times being what they are) you may be graciously disposed to restore this work, and my most respectful petition is by no means directed towards securing the immediate and complete re-establishment of our Chapel but, as I said, towards saving it from speedy and evident ruin and, as it were, to preserve a seed of our orchestra – the which, according to my humble ideas and reflections, could most conveniently be done by recruiting the following boys, bringing them together feeding them and training them in music.

Firstly

Four choir – or singing-boys...

Moreover

Four instrumentalist-boys...

This, most gracious Elector, is in my humble estimate the proper and most befitting means by which Your Serene Highness can not only to some extent preserve your Court Chapel and enjoy a little music at your table, but also, when better times return – as please God they soon will – by adding a few good Italian or other instruments and as many good singers whenever you may be graciously pleased, you can complete and enlarge the Collegium Musicum, which, without the preparation I now most humbly propose and bring to your recollection, can scarce be hoped for.

There can be no doubt that Your Serene Highness will give gracious approval to my respectful proposal and put the same into effect; you will thus be giving further proof of the considerable prerogatives you possess... And who knows but that Your Serene Highness, among your present heavy cares of government, may in this manner be sometimes refreshed in spirit and the more richly blest by the good God with lasting health and other marks of prosperity befitting a prince...

He next wrote to the son of the Elector, Prince Christian of Saxony, pleading for help for the musicians who were destitute and in ill-health.

SCHÜTZ TO PRINCE CHRISTIAN OF SAXONY

Dresden,
14 August 1651

...Most gracious Lord: reluctant though I am to burden so illustrious a Prince with my repeated letters and reminders, yet I am compelled thereto by the continual comings and goings, hour after hour, the exceeding great lamentation, wretchedness and moaning of all the company of the poor, neglected musicians of the Chapel, who are living in such distress as would draw tears from a stone in the ground. May God be my witness that their wretched condition and piteous lamentation pierces my heart, since I know not how to give them comfort and hope of some relief.

In former days one would scarce have thought it possible, but most of the company are firmly resolved and say that sooner than bring discredit upon their most gracious Lord by begging their bread, they will set out, compelled by dire necessity, and go their ways elsewhere; that it is impossible for them to remain and continue to endure what they have had to suffer for so long, they must perforce depart, leaving anyone who will to pay their debts. They have had enough of insults, no one will any longer give them credit for a groat, etc.

The duty I owe to my most gracious Elector and Lord obliges me, in view of this necessity, to submit the matter to the notice of Your Princely Highness, as our most gracious Inspector and master, and to bring to your most gracious consideration that it would be a pitiful thing if the company, assembled with great pains and labour, were to be thus broken up and scattered.

I therefore submit to Your Princely Highness my most humble, earnest plea that you may compassionately solicit His Serene Highness, as your dearly beloved Father, to allow but a single quarter's salary to be paid to the company, that it may at least be held together.

And for this reason most graciously to inform me whether some little comfort or hope may be given them; that they may not be left in want and obliged to seek their bread elsewhere. But if Your Princely Highness should be unable to make some beneficial arrangement – though that is against all my hope – it would be impossible for me to hold them longer. In such case I shall have done my best and have no blame...

Schütz continues to be beset with problems.

Dresden

28 May 1652

....These 3 weeks past I have been unable to go out because of the flux in my head which, if you will excuse me, later affected both my thighs and turned to erysipelas*, but I had long ago agreed to this and now cannot conceal from you that the bass (Georg Kaiser, member of the Court Chapel), who from poverty again pawned his clothes a while ago, since when he has dwelt in his house in a state of brutishness, like a wild beast in the forest, is now again bestirring himself and informs me through his wife, that he must and will leave this place...

Yet it would be infinite pity to lose so fine a voice from the Chapel. What matter that in other respects his disposition is none too good and that his tongue requires daily washing in the wine-tankard – it is only that so wide a gullet needs more moistening than several narrow ones, and even if the good fellow received his slender wages regularly, they would not stretch to great banquets; and with a right understanding of the fellow's management and housekeeping one should, to my mind, merely give him his small due at the proper time; but as long as this is not done, he cannot fairly be decried as a great spendthrift...

> Schutz carried on working to the end of his life and although his requests to be pensioned off were ignored, he did see the gradual recovery of his devastated country and of the Chapel for which he had worked so hard.

---

*an inflammation of the skin causing pain and swelling, more common in those days, particularly when one was run-down.

JEAN-BAPTISTE LULLY
1632 – 1687

Lully was born in Florence, where, in spite of his humble birth, he somehow learnt to play the guitar. He was noticed by the Chevalier de Guise and at fourteen went to Paris into the service of Mademoiselle d'Orleans a cousin of the Chevalier. He soon became well known at Court for his violin playing and dancing and at twenty he entered the service of Louis XIV. In 1653 he was appointed composer of dance music and quickly became a favourite of the King and a very powerful man at Court. He secured from the King a national monopoly of opera writing and production, and became resident composer at Versailles.

He was a master of intrigue and string-pulling and showed no generosity towards fellow artists; such was his jealousy towards the success of potential rivals that he had them imprisoned by petitioning the King. Even one of his close friends, Molière, fell foul of his scheming.

Lully, however, did bring to the French opera a distinctive style and he developed the Academie Royale de Musique which, as the Paris Opera, has remained the most prominent musical institution in France.

Lully is remembered for dying from an abscess caused by putting his conducting baton through his foot while conducting a Te Deum.

In the following letter he refers to one of his intrigues in the business of snatching the Royal privilege from its previous holders.

LULLY TO JEAN-BAPTISTE COLBERT

Paris,
3 June 1672

Monseigneur,

Since I had the honour of speaking to you about the Royal Academy of Music, I have been daily subjected to further annoyances, of which I make bold to send you the latest, whereby you shall know, Monseigneur, that they make *false declarations* in everything, and in the first place when they say that they obtained the Letters Patent from the King in the name of Perrin; and in the second place by declaring that I took the King by surprise, they who have presented several petitions to His Majesty and who knew his intentions better than I did. You know, Monseigneur, that I have followed no other course in this matter *than that which you prescribed to me*, and that at the beginning I believed they would follow the same. But they were careful not to submit themselves to your judgement, well knowing *that you would tolerate no imposture of the sort they have in mind* and which they intend to enforce in Parliament, *and with which you are more familiar than anyone in the world...*

I hope, Monseigneur, that through your kindness the King will grant me the theatre in the Louvre, in which I would have work begun at once, despite the annoyances of the lawsuit, and would have the honour of waiting upon you with N. Quinault to show you a project for the King's return, which I do not doubt will be brought to success, if it finds your approval...

> Lully was granted the Royal privilege and opened his theatre in the autumn, but very soon found he needed to make improvements to the building.

LULLY TO JEAN-BAPTISTE COLBERT

Paris,
July 1673

M. Colbert is most humbly begged to inform the King that the Royal Academy of Music requests His Majesty's permission to raise the ceiling of that part of the theatre in the Palais Royal which is above the stage, a thing which can be done without disturbing the roof of the said Palace or touching any of the apartments in the theatre. It also asks that certain beams which are broken and threaten to collapse, may be changed before work can begin, by reason that it would be unsafe to set up machinery there.

On either side of the proscenium there are two stone pillars which serve no purpose but, on the contrary, greatly encumber the space for the scenery. His Majesty is most humbly begged to grant permission to remove these and to use the stone to raise the walls, in the manner aforementioned. The whole on condition that the building and the measures proposed shall first be inspected by the officials of His Majesty's buildings and approved by Mons. Colbert. The Academy being at present under the necessity of paying for the subsistence of the Italian comedians and defraying the expense of building the new theatre, as well as the salaries and ordinary allowances of the Academicians, all this expense is so great that it most humbly begs His Majesty to consider that its establishment or its ruin depends entirely on a new play in the Palais Royal before the winter...

> His request was granted.

GEORGE FREDERICK HANDEL
1685 – 1759

Handel was born in Halle in Germany but settled in England in 1712. He was already well known as an operatic composer in Germany and Italy, and he quickly made his fortune in London. The political structure in England was very different from that in Europe. In England the aristocracy and wealthy gentry were as important patrons of the arts as the King. Opera remained Handel's central preoccupation for many years. He organised yearly a season which lasted several months and for which he used prominent singers, mostly recruited from Italy. This letter shows how well paid some of them were.

HANDEL TO FRANCIS COLMAN (BRITISH AMBASSADOR TO THE COURT OF TUSCANY)

London,
27 October 1730

Monsieur,

I have just been honoured with your letter of the 22nd last, from which I see the reasons that determined you to engage Sr Senesino on the footing of fourteen hundred Guineas, in which we acquiesce; and I most humbly thank you for the pains you have been good enough to take in this matter. The said Sr Senesino arrived here 12 days ago and I did not fail on presentation of your letter to pay him on account of his salary the hundred Guineas you had promised him. As for Sigra Pisani, we have not had her, and as the season is now far advanced and the operas will soon begin, we shall dispense with any other women from Italy this year, having already arranged the operas for the company we have at present.

I am, however, much obliged to you for having thought of Sigra Maddalena Pieri, in case we had had absolute need of another woman to take men's parts, but we shall rest content with the five persons, having now found means of making up what was lacking.

It is to your generous assistance that the Court and the Nobility will in part owe the satisfaction of now having a company to their taste, so that it only remains for me to express to you my particular gratitude for this and to assure you of the most respectful attention, etc., etc.,

During his management of the opera seasons in London Handel became embroiled in the rivalry between the Italian singers and operatic competitors. This eventually forced him into bankruptcy. He abandoned opera and thereafter concentrated on the writing of oratorios.

Charles Jennens, one of his patrons and admirers, also helped with the libretti of some of Handel's oratorios, including the *Messiah, Saul* and *Belshazzar*. Handel's letters to him show a delight that such an influential patron should also write such sympathetic libretti.

The following letter was written shortly after the first performance of *Messiah*.

HANDEL TO CHARLES JENNENS

Dublin,
29 December 1741

Sir,

It was with the greatest pleasure I saw the continuation of your kindness by the lines you were pleased to send me, in order to be prefixed to your oratorio *Messiah*, which I set to music before I left England. I am emboldened, Sir, by the generous concern you please to take in relation to my affairs, to give you an account of the success I have met here. The Nobility did me the honour to make amongst themselves a subscription for 6 nights, which did fill a room of 600 persons, so that I needed not sell one single ticket at the door. And without vanity the performance was received with general approbation. Sig^ra Avoglio, which I brought with me from London, pleases extraordinary. I have found another tenor voice which gives great satisfaction. The basses and counter tenors are very good, and the rest of the chorus singers (by my direction) do exceeding well; as for the instruments, they are really excellent, Mr Dubourg being at the head of them, and the music sounds delightfully in this charming room, which puts me in such spirits (and my health being so good), that I exert myself on my organ with more than usual success. I opened with the *Allegro, Penseroso & Moderato*, and I assure you that the words of the *Moderato* are vastly admired. The audience being composed (besides the flowers of ladies of distinction and other people of the greatest quality) of so many bishops, deans, heads of the college, the most eminent people in the Law as the Chancellor, Auditor General, etc., all of which are very much taken with the poetry. So that I am desired to perform it again the next time. I cannot sufficiently express the kind treatment I receive here, but the politeness of this generous nation cannot be unknown to you, so I let you judge of the satisfaction I enjoy, passing my time with honour, profit and pleasure. They propose already to have some more performances when the 6 nights of the subscription are over...

Handel again turned to his collaborator, Charles Jennens.

9th June 1744

It gave me great Pleasure to hear Your safe arrival in the Country, and that Your Health was much improved. I hope it is by this time firmly established, and I wish You with all my Heart the Continuation of it, and all the Prosperity. As You do me the Honour to encourage my Musical undertakings, and even to promote them with a particular kindness, I take the Liberty to trouble you with an account of what Engagements I have hitherto concluded. I have taken the Opera House in the Haymarket, engaged, as Singers, Signora Francesina, Mr Robinson, Beard, Reinhold, Mr Gates with his Boyes's and several of the best Chorus Singers from the choirs, and I have some hopes that Mrs Cibber will sing for me. She sent word from Bath (where she is now) that she would perform for me next Winter with great pleasure if it did not interfere with her playing, but I think I can obtain Mr Riches's permission (with whom she is engaged to play in Covent Garden House) since so obligingly he gave Leave to Mr Beard and Mr Reinhold. Now should I be extremely glad to receive the first Act, or what is ready, of the new Oratorio with which you intend to favour me, that I might employ all my attention and time, in order to answer in some measure the great Obligation I lay under. This new favour will greatly increase my Obligations.

The new oratorio was *Belshazzar*. He then started work on *Hercules* and in the following letter written to Charles Jennens on the 19th July, he worries about its length.

At my arrival in London, which was yesterday, I immediately perused the Act of the Oratorio with which you favour'd me, and, the little time only I had it, gives me great Pleasure. Your reasons for the Length of the first act are entirely Satisfactory to me, and it is likewise my Opinion to have the following Acts short. I shall be very glad and much obliged to you, if you will soon favour me with the remaining Acts. Be pleased to point out these passages in the Messiah which You think require altering...

A month later (21 August), having just completed *Hercules*, he wrote again asking for the libretto third act of *Belshazzar*:

The Second Act of the Oratorio; I have received Safe, and own my self highly obliged to You for it. I am greatly pleased with it, and shall use my best endeavours to do it Justice. I can only Say that I impatiently wait for the third Act...

Again, on 13th September, he requests the words for the third act. This letter also reveals Handel's attention to detail and his enthusiasm for using the chorus to its best advantage.

Your most excellent Oratorio has given me great Delight in setting it to Musick and still engages me warmly. It is indeed a Noble Piece, very grand and uncommon, it has furnished me with Expressions, and has given me Opportunity to some very particular Ideas, besides so many great Choruses. I entreat you heartily to favour me soon with the last Act, which I expect with anxiety, that I may regulate my Self the better as to the Length of it. I profess my Self highly obliged to you, for so generous a Present...

In the next letter he proposes cutting some of the ceremonial choruses.

I received the 3rd Act, with a great deal of pleasure, as you can imagine, and you may believe that I think it a very fine and sublime Oratorio, only it is really too long, if I should extend the Musick, it would last 4 Hours and more. I retrench'd already a great deal of the Musick, that I might preserve the Poetry as much as I could, yet still it may be shortned. The Anthems come in very properly, but would not the Words (tell it out among the Heathen that the Lord is King.) [be] sufficient for one Chorus? Te Anthem (I will magnify thee O God my King, and I will praise thy name for ever and ever, vers). the Lord preserveth all them that love him, but scattreth abroad all the ungodly. (vers and Chorus) my mouth shall speak the Praise of the Lord and let all flesh give thanks unto His holy name for ever and ever Amen) concludes well the Oratorio. I hope you will make a Visit to London next Winter. I have a good Set of Singers. Sr Francesina performs Nitocris, Miss Robinson, Cyrus, Mrs Cibber, Daniel, Mr Beard (who is recoverd) Belshazzar, Mr Reinhold, Gobrias, and a good Number of Choir Singers for the Chorus's. I propose 24 Nights to perform this Season on Saturdays but in Lent on Wednesday's or fryday's. I shall open Ye 3d of Novembr next with Deborah.

JOHANN SEBASTIAN BACH
1685–1750

Although Bach went to Halle in 1729 to meet Handel who was on a brief visit to his birthplace, he arrived too late, and so the two greatest musicians of their time, born in the same year and not too distant from each other, never met. Their careers, however, were very different. Whilst Handel travelled frequently throughout Europe with the lavish support of the King and nobility of England, Bach spent his whole life in the drab confines of provincial cites in Germany, impoverished by the Thirty Years War. Bach first served at the Court of the Duke of Weimar before moving to the Court of the Prince of Anhalt in Cöthen. Here he was also Cantor, in charge of the St. Thomas-Schule and of music in the churches of St. Thomas and St. Nicolai, in Leipzig. Unlike Handel and many other composers, he did not have social contacts .

It is difficult to accept that the genius Bach was regarded merely as a craftsman and was expected to undertake the roles of teacher, composer, performer and choirmaster.

In the following document Bach pledges his service to the Leipzig Town Council.

UNDERTAKING OF THE CANTOR AT AT THOMAS'S SCHOOL

1 That I shall set the boys the good example of an honourable, disciplined way of life, watch zealously over the school and faithfully instruct the boys,

2 To the best of my ability, bring the music in both the parish churches of this town into a good state,

3 Show all due respect and obedience to the honourable Council, watching over and furthering its honour and reputation in all places as well as may be; likewise, should a gentleman of the Council desire the boys to take part in a performance, that I shall permit them to go to him without opposition, but that apart from this I shall in no circumstances allow them to go into the country for funerals or weddings without the knowledge and consent of the Burgomaster in office and the headmaster of the school,

4 Give due obedience to the inspector and headmaster of the school in all such matters as they may order on behalf of the honourable Council,

5 Take no boy into the school unless he already has a grounding in music or unless he comes with the purpose of receiving instruction in the matter...,

6 Instruct the boys zealously, not in singing only, but also in instrumental music, that the churches may not be burdened with unnecessary expense,

7 In maintaining good order in the churches, so arrange the music that it shall not last over-long, and shall be of a style which will not produce an *operatic* effect, but rather encourage the listeners to piety,

8 Provide the New Church with good scholars,

9 Deal with the boys in a friendly and circumspect manner, but should any refuse obedience, punish them in *moderation* or report them to the proper quarter,

10 Be faithful in providing instruction in the school, and in all matters pertaining thereto,

11 And if I should be unable to do this myself, arrange for it to be done by another able *subjectum* at no cost to the honourable Council or the school,

12 Not go outside the town without the permission of the Burgo-master in office,

13 At all funerals, according to custom, walk with and beside the boys as much as possible,

14 And not accept any *Officium* at the University without the *Consens* of the honourable Council,

as I hereby, and by virtue of the foregoing, undertake and pledge myself faithfully to comply with the same and not to act in a contrary manner, on pain of the loss of my employment. In token whereof I have signed this undertaking with my own hand, etc., etc.

Bach, who was proud, determined and at times irascible, soon found himself at odds with the authorities, partly because of his claim to the directorship of music in the University, which his predecessors had held, and partly because he was not suited to be the subordinate to a musically ignorant town council. This is expressed in his few surviving personal letters written to an influential friend, George Erdmann, the Russian Plenipotentiary at Danzig.

BACH TO GEORGE ERDMANN

Leipzig,
28 October 1730

...Almost 4 years have now gone by since your Honour favoured me with a kind reply to my letter; and remembering that you were graciously pleased to ask for some news of my misfortunes, I herewith obediently comply with that request. You are well acquainted with my fate from youth up, until the change took me to Cöthen as conductor. There I found a benevolent Prince, with a love and knowledge of music, and thought to pass the rest of my life in his service. But as it so fell out, the said Serene Highness married a princess of Berenburg, and it seemed thereafter that the said Prince's inclination for music had somewhat cooled, especially as the new Princess appeared to be an *amusa*; and it so pleased God that I should be offered a position here as *Directore musices* and *Cantore* at St. Thomas's School. At first, indeed, I felt it most unbecoming to change from conductor to cantor. I therefore delayed my decision for some three months; but the post was so favourably described to me that in the end (particularly as my sons seemed disposed towards *studiis*) I took courage in the name of the All Highest and went to Leipzig, passed my examination and accepted the change. By God's will I have been here ever since. As, however, (1) I find that this service is not near so lucrative as it had been described to me, (2) many *Accidentia* [perquisites] of the post escaped me, (3) the place is very expensive and (4) the authorities are hard to please and care little for music, so that I am obliged to live amid almost continual vexation, envy and persecution, it seems that I shall be compelled, with your gracious assistance, to seek my *Fortune* elsewhere. Should your honour know of or discover any *convenable station* for an old and faithful servant in that place, I would respectfully beg you to vouch for me a gracious *Recommendation*; and I for my part shall make my best endeavour to give satisfaction for your gracious testimonial and intercession. My present post brings in about 700 thalers, and when there are a few more funerals than *ordinairement*, the perquisites increase proportionately; but when the air is wholesome, on the contrary, they diminish, this last year my *ordinaire* perquisites for burials declined by more than 100 thalers. In Thuringia I can make make 400 thalers go further than twice as many hundred in this place, owing to the excessively high cost of living.   I have married again, my first wife having died in peace in Cöthen. From my first marriage, 3 sons and one daughter survive. From my second marriage one son and two daughters. My eldest son is a *studiosus juris*, the other two still respectively frequent *primam* and *secundam classem*, and my eldest daughter is still unmarried. The children of the other marriage are still young, the eldest, the boy, being 6 years old. All of them however are born *Musici* and I can assure you that I am already able to form a concert *vocaliter* and *instumentaliter* from my own family, as my wife sings a very pretty *soprano* and my eldest daughter too, joins in not badly...

> Nevertheless, Bach stayed in Leipzig, where he remained restless and dissatisfied. He continued to write a series of masterpieces for the church – his passions, cantatas, motets, choral-preludes – which all seemed beyond the appreciation of the citizens of Leipzig. This work remained hidden amongst his manuscripts until discovered a century later. In 1733 Bach petitioned for the position of Court Composer to the King of Poland and Elector of Saxony. With the application, Bach dedicated to the King the Kyrie and Gloria from his *Mass in B minor*.

Dresden,
27 July 1733
...With the deepest devotion I offer your Royal Majesty the present trifling example of the skill I have attained in Music, most humbly begging that you will not judge it by its bad composition, but in your world-famous clemency will look graciously upon it and deign to take me into your most mighty protection.

> On a personal level Bach continued with determination to fight for his financial dues as Head of Music in the cathedral.

BACH TO THE TOWN COUNCIL, LEIPZIG

Leipzig,
25 August 1733
Magnificent, most honourable, learned and wise, most honoured gentlemen and distinguished patrons.
May it please you to condescend to hear how Herr Johann Fredrich Eitelwein, merchant of this town, was married on 12 August of the present year

out of town, and therefore believes himself entitled to withhold the fees due to us in such cases, and has made bold to disregard many friendly reminders from us. Whereas the said fees make up the greater part of our emoluments, and no one has hitherto endeavoured to withhold them from us. We are therefore compelled most dutifully to beg you, most magnificent and honourable gentlemen, for this reason to take us under your protection and by your decision and care to uphold us in our old rights and agreed *Salario*, and further to enjoin upon the said Herr Eitelwein that he remit to us our lawful shares of the marriage fees, to each his due proportion, together with the costs occasioned, in this instance, which we also claim, with all fitting respect and reverence.

Your magnificent and honourable gentlemen, our most honoured Lords and distinguished Patrons,

from your most dutifully devoted
Johann Sebastian Bach,
Director of Music and Cantor,
Johannes Schneider, Organist,
M. Johann Matthis Gesner, Rector of St. Thomas's School,
on behalf of the Alumni of that School

CHRISTOPH WILLIBALD GLUCK
1714 – 1787

Gluck was born in Bavaria, but his early twenties and thirties were spent writing operas, first in Italy and then in London. He travelled extensively throughout Europe, writing and producing new operas before becoming resident in Vienna (1749-73), then in Paris (1773-9). He finally returned to Vienna in 1779.

The music of Gluck was very different from that of Bach with its expressiveness and lightness characterising the new music of the mid-eighteenth century. Although it seems unlikely that Gluck had heard any of Monteverdi's music, they used the same base of ancient dramas for their operas.

Gluck was the first great musician to realize the enormous importance of public opinion in promoting success and fame. He was very careful to cultivate his public and his publicity.

He too was dependent on patronage, which he found in the Imperial family in Vienna. He was their music teacher and one of his pupils was the Archduchess Marie Antoinette, who married Louis XVI of France. It was through this connection that he went to the Academie Royale de Musique in Paris, the most distinguished opera theatre in Europe. There he set about reforming the style of opera. He was always in the news, particularly in connection with his rival, the Italian composer Nicola Piccinni.

Duke Don Giovanni di Braganza, Gluck's correspondent in this first letter, was described by the music historian Charles Burney in his Diary of a musical journey, (1773) as 'an excellent judge of music... a great traveller, having visited England, France and Italy before his arrival in Germany. He is very lively, and occasioned much mirth by his pleasantries, which were all seasoned with good humour.'

GLUCK TO DUKE DON GIOVANNI DI BRAGANZA

Vienna,
30th October 1770

Highness!

In dedicating my latest work to Your Highness, I crave not so much a protector as a judge. A spirit secure against the prejudices of habit, a sufficient knowledge of the great principles of art, a taste formed not so much on great models as on the immutable foundations of beauty and truth, these are the attributes which I seek in my Maecenas and which I find united in Your Highness. The sole reason that induced me to publish my music for *Alceste* was the hope of finding imitators who, spurred on by the full support of an enlightened public, would follow the new trail and would summon the courage to eliminate the abuses which have crept into the Italian theatre and bring it as near perfection as possible. I reproach myself for having thus far attempted to do this in vain. The demi-savants and professors of taste, whose number is unhappily legion and who represent the greatest barrier to artistic progress, have come out in opposition to a method which, if it should gain a footing, would destroy at once all their pretensions as critics and as creators. They believed they could pass judgement on *Alceste* after chaotic, badly directed and even more badly executed rehearsals; the attempt was made to gauge in a room the effect produced in a theatre, with the same ingenuity as was once employed in a city in Greece to judge statues, which were intended to stand on lofty columns, from a few feet away. One delicate ear found an air too harsh or a transition too forceful and badly prepared, without pausing to consider that full force of expression and maximum contrast were called for. One pedantic harmonist took advantage of a judicious oversight or a fault in the score to denounce the one and the other as unpardonable sins against the mysteries of harmony; and then voices were raised in unison against this allegedly barbarous and extravagant music.

It is true that other scores have been judged by the same criterion, and judgement on them is given with no less assurance; but Your Highness can easily see the reason for this. The more one seeks truth and perfection, the more necessary it is to be precise and exact. The qualities which distinguish Raphael from a dozen other painters are imperceptible, and, any alteration of contour, which might be permissible in caricature, would wholly disfigure the portrait of a beautiful woman. Little or nothing, apart from a slight alteration in the mode of expression, would be needed to turn my aria in *Orfeo*, *Che faro senze Euridice?* into a puppet-dance. One note more or less sustained, failure to increase the tempo or make the voice louder, one appoggiatura out of place, a trill, a passage or roulade, can ruin a whole scene in such an opera. And when it is a question of executing music written according to the principles I have laid down, the presence of the composer is, so to speak, as necessary as the presence of the sun to the works of nature. He is the absolute life and soul, and without him everything remains in confusion and darkness. But one must be prepared for these obstacles as long as one lives in the same world with people who feel they have the authority to judge the fine arts just because they are privileged to possess a pair of eyes and a pair of ears, no matter which. It is unhappily an all too common mistake amongst men, this mania for talking of things they least understand...

GLUCK TO THE COUNTESS VON FRIES

Paris,
16 November 1777

Madame.

I have been so plagued about music, and am so much disgusted with it that at present I would not write one single note for a louis; by this you may conceive, madame, the degree of my devotion to you, since I have been able to bring myself to arrange the two songs for the harp for you, and have the honour to send them herewith. Never has a more terrible and keenly-contested *battaglia* been waged, than the one I began with my opera *Armide*. The cabals against *Iphigenie*, *Orfeo* and *Alceste* were no more than little skirmishes of light horse by comparison. The Neapolitan Ambassador, to ensure great success for Piccinni's opera, is tirelessly intriguing against me, at Court and among the nobility. He has induced Marmontel, La Harpe and several members of the Academy to write against my system of music and my manner of composing. The Abbe Arnaud, M. Suard and several others have come to my defence, and the quarrel grew so heated that from insults they would have passed to blows, but that friends of both sides brought them to order. The *Journal de Paris* which comes out every day, is full of it. This dispute is making the Editor's fortune, for he already has more than 2,500 subscribers in Paris. That's the musical revolution in France, amid the most brilliant pomp. Enthusiasts tell me: Sir, you are fortunate to be enjoying the honour of persecution; every great genius has had the same experience. – I wish them to the devil with their fine speeches. The fact is that the opera, which was said to have fallen flat, brought in 37,200 *livres* in 7 performances, without counting the boxes rented for the year, and without the subscribers. Yesterday, at the 8th performance, they took 5,767 *livres*...The pit was so tightly packed that when a man who had his hat on his head was told by the· guard to take it off, he replied: 'Come and take it off yourself, for I cannot move my arms'; which caused laughter. I have seen people coming out with their hair bedraggled and their clothes drenched as though they had fallen into a stream. Only Frenchmen would pay so dearly for a pleasure. There are passages in the opera which force the audience to lose their countenance and their composure. Come yourself, Madame, to witness the tumult; it will amuse you as much as the opera...

JOSEF HAYDN
1732–1809

Born in Austria and made destitute as an adolescent, Josef Haydn was forced by his poverty to accept employment from Prince Esterhazy at Eisenstadt, far out in the countryside of the Austro-Hungarian borderland. Despite having to compose to order he brought a liveliness and creativity to his music, as well as considerable energy, developing and firmly establishing, among others, the forms of string quartet and symphony.

The following letter shows his generosity towards his fellow composer, Mozart.

He met him on one of his visits to Vienna with the Prince. These trips were very important to him as a way of meeting music-lovers and fellow musicians. Mozart regarded Haydn as the only contemporary musician from whom he could still learn.

HAYDN TO PROVINZIALOBERVERWALTER ROTH (PRAGUE)

December 1787

...You ask me for an Opera buffa. With the greatest pleasure, if you would care to have an example of my compositions for singers to keep to yourself. But I can be of no service to you at the moment in presenting them on the stage in Prague for all my Operas are too closely connected with our company [at Esterhaz in Hungary], and elsewhere they would never produce the effect that I have calculated with that place in mind. It would be a quite different matter were I to have the supreme good fortune to compose an entirely new libretto for that Theatre [at Prague]. But that too would be very venturesome, since it is hard for anyone to stand beside the great Mozart.

For if I could but impress the matchless works of Mozart upon the souls of all music-lovers, and particularly of the Great, so deeply and with such understanding and sensibility as that with which I myself appreciate, and comprehend them, the Nations would vie with one another to possess such a treasure within their walls. Prague must hold the dear fellow – but reward him too; for without that, the history of great geniuses is melancholy and gives posterity little encouragement to further effort; on which account, alas, so many promising minds fall short of fulfilment. It angers me that the peerless Mozart has not yet been engaged at an imperial or royal court! Forgive me if I am carried away; but I am so fond of the man...

> Back in the country he missed Vienna. He writes with nostalgia to a musical friend and wealthy patron of the arts. They are to strike up a regular correspondence.

Esterhaz,
9 February 1790

Dear Frau v. Genzinger,

Now – here I sit in my wilderness – deserted – like a poor orphan – almost without human company – sad – full of the memory of precious days gone by – yes, alas, gone by – and who knows when those pleasant days will return again? that charming company? wherein a whole circle shares One heart, One soul – all those fine musical evenings – which can only be remembered, not described in writing – where is all that enthusiasm? Gone – and gone for a long time. Your Grace must not be surprised that I have been so long in writing you my thanks! At home I found everything in confusion and for 3 days I did not know whether I was *Kapell-master* or *Kapell-servant*, nothing could comfort me, my whole apartment was in disorder, my Forte-piano, which I used to love, was out of order, disobedient, it rather vexed than soothed me, I got little sleep, even my dreams were a persecution, for when I dreamt that I was hearing an excellent performance of *Le Nozze di Figaro* that odious north wind woke me and almost blew my nightcap off my head. In 3 days I lost 20 pounds in weight, for the good Viennese titbits had already disappeared during the journey. Yes, yes, thought I to myself as I sat in my boarding-house, obliged to eat a piece off a 50-year-old cow instead of that delicious beef, an ancient mutton-stew with yellow turnips instead of the ragout with little dumplings, a slice of roast leather instead of the Bohemian pheasant, a so-called *Dschabl* or *Gros-Salat* instead of those delicious, delicate oranges, tough apple-rings and hazelnuts instead of those pastries – and so forth. Yes, yes, thought I to myself, if only I had here all those titbits I could not manage to eat at Vienna! – Here at Esterhaz nobody asks me – do you take chocolate with milk or without, would you like coffee, black or with cream, what can I get you, my dear Haydn, would you like vanilla ice or a pineapple one? If only I had here a piece of good Parmesan cheese, especially on fast days to help the black dumplings and noodles down more easily, – this very day I ordered our porter to send me down a few pounds of it.

Forgive me, dearest lady, if on this first occasion I waste your time with such preposterous stuff in my wretched scribbling; forgive me as a man to whom the Viennese were too kind; but I am already gradually beginning to get used to country ways, yesterday I did some studying for the first time and it was quite in the Haydn manner.

You will certainly have been more diligent than I. The agreeable Adagio from the Quartet has, I hope, already been given its true expression by your lovely fingers. My dear Fraulein Peperl [daughter of Frau von Gensinger] will (I hope) often sing the Cantata and thus remember her Master, especially in clear expression and precise vocalization, for it would be a crime for such a beautiful voice to remain hidden in her breast, so I beg for a frequent smile, otherwise I shall take it amiss. I commend myself to Mons. Francois (her son) likewise for his musical talent. Even if he does sing in his dressing-gown it always goes well, I shall often send something new to encourage him. Meanwhile I kiss your hand again for all your kindness to me, and remain, my life long, with greatest respect etc...

HAYDN TO FRAU VON GENZINGER

Esterhaz,
14 March 1790

I beg your gracious pardon a million times for my tardiness in answering your two letters, which gave me so much pleasure. The cause was not negligence (from which sin Heaven will preserve me all my life), but the many matters I have to attend to for my most gracious Prince in his present sad situation. The death of his late wife so much depressed the Prince that we were all obliged to devote our energies to rousing him from his grief. For the first three evenings I therefore arranged large concerts of chamber music, but with no singing. But on hearing the first music, the poor Prince fell into such melancholy over my Favorit-Adagio in D, that I had a hard task to bring him out of it with other pieces.

By the fourth day we were already playing Opera, on the fifth a Comedy, and finally, the daily performance as usual; at the same time I gave order for the study of the old Opera by Gassmann, *L'amor artigiano*, because our master had remarked shortly before that he would like to see it. I wrote three new Arias for it, which I will send you by the next post, not because they are beautiful, but in order to convince you, gracious Lady, of my diligence... It enraptures me to learn that my dear Arianna [Haydn's cantata, *Arianna a Naxos*] is winning applause at Schottenhof [the home of the Genzinger family]; I would just like to remind Fraulein Peperl to pronounce the words clearly, particularly in *Chi tanto amai*...

In 1790 Prince Nicolaus Esterhazy died. His successor dissolved the band and granted Haydn a comfortable pension. He decided to accept the invitation of the impresario J.P. Salomon and went on two trips to London in 1791 and 1794. There, he found that he was a celebrity and it was during this time that he wrote his last twelve symphonies and his two oratorios, *The Creation* and *The Seasons*, both with libretti of English origin. They were Haydn's response to the overwhelming impression made on him by performances of Handel's oratorios.

HAYDN TO FRAU VON GENZINGER

London
8 January 1791

...I hope, gracious Madam, that you will have received my last letter from Calais. I ought indeed to have sent a report as soon as I reached London, as I had promised, only I desired to wait for a few days that I might write of several matters together. I therefore report that on the first of this month, viz. New Year's Day, at half-past seven in the morning, after attending Mass, I went on board ship and, thanks be to the Almighty, reached Dover safe and sound at 5 o'clock in the afternoon...

During the entire crossing I remained on deck, in order to sate my eyes with that monstrous animal, the sea. So long as there was no wind, I was not afraid, but finally as the wind grew ever stronger and I saw the high unruly waves breaking against the ship, I felt a little alarm, and with it a little nausea. However, I overcame it all and, *salva venia*, came safely into the harbour without vomiting. Most people were sick, and looked like ghosts. I took two days to recover. But now I am quite brisk and merry again, and am looking at London, that vast city which quite amazes me by its various beauties and wonders. I at once paid the necessary calls, visiting, among others, the Neapolitan Ambassador and our own. Both of them returned by call two days later, and four days ago I took my midday meal at the house of the former, but *nota bene* at 6 o'clock in the evening. Such is the fashion here...

My arrival made a great stir all over the town. For 3 days I was bandied about in all the papers. Everyone is curious to meet me. I have already been obliged to eat out 5 times, and might be invited every day if I would, but I must consider first my health and 2. my work. Except for the Mylords I receive no visitors until 2 o'clock in the afternoon, at 4 o'clock I eat at home with Mon. Salomon...I have a small, convenient but costly lodging. My landlord is an Italian, and a cook as well, he serves me 4 very good meals, we pay 1 fl. 30 kr. each per day, without wine and beer, but everything is terribly dear. Yesterday I went to a big amateur concert, but I arrived rather too late, and when I handed over my ticket they would not let me in, but led me into a neighbouring room where I had to remain until the piece then being performed in the hall was over. They then opened the doors and I was led, on the arm of the Manager, amid general hand-clapping, down the middle of the hall to the front of the pit, where I was gaped at and admired with a host of English compliments. People assured me that this honour had not been shown to anyone for 50 years. After the concert I was taken to another fine room next to the hall, where a large table enough to take 200 people stood ready for the whole company of amateurs, with a great number of places laid, and they desired me to sit at the head of it. Only, as I had that very day dined out and eaten more than usual, I refused this honour, with the excuse that I felt a little unwell, despite which, however, I had to drink in Burgundy wine to the harmonious health of all those present, who returned the toast, and then they allowed me to be driven home. All this was very flattering for me, yet I wished I might escape to Vienna for a little while, to work in greater quiet, for the noise in the streets, from all the various tradesfolk, is intolerable. True, I am as yet still engaged on symphonic work, because the libretto for the opera is not yet decided upon, but for the sake of quiet I shall have to take a room right outside the town...

On 9 December 1791 Mozart died in Vienna. The news reached London a fortnight later.

London,
20 December 1791

...Now, dear lady, I would like to quarrel with you a little because you believe I prefer the city of London to Vienna and enjoy being here more than in my own country. I do not dislike London, but I could not bear to spend the rest of my days there, even if I could earn millions. The reason for this I will tell you by word of mouth. I am as happy as a child at the thought of returning home to embrace my good friends. My only regret will be at not including the great Mozart, if it be true, as I hope it is not, that he is dead. The world will not have such a talent again in a hundred years!

HAYDN TO MICHAEL PUCHBERG (A FRIEND OF MOZART'S IN VIENNA)

London,
January 1792

...I was quite beside myself for a long while because of his [Mozart's] death, and could not believe that Providence would have so rapidly despatched an irreplaceable man to the other world, I only regret that he could not first have convinced the English, who are still in the dark, of what I had been daily preaching to them...

WOLFGANG AMADEUS MOZART
1756–1791

Mozart was born in Salzburg on the 27th January 1756, the son of highly musical parents, Leopold and Marianne. His father was a violinist, a minor composer and a court musician at Salzburg in the service of the Archbishop Sigismund von Schrattenbach. Mozart was already composing at the age of seven but he was better known for his playing and his father organized extensive concert tours of Europe to supplement his own meagre income.

Mozart's letters are in turn expressive, straightforward, intelligent and wily. It says something about his energy that besides composing symphonies, concertos, operas and oratorios and a wealth of chamber works, he still had time to write a large number of letters to his family and friends revealing the many facets of his personality. Not only do we get glimpses of the child prodigy, the spoilt or unstable musician, but also of the loving friend and caring son and brother. He is also adept at turning on the persuasion when necessary, such as when he badly needs a job.

MOZART TO HIS MOTHER AND SISTER

Bologna
21 August 1770

I too am still alive and, what is more, as merry as can be. I had a great desire to-day to ride on a donkey, for it is the custom in Italy, and so I thought that I too should try it. We have the honour to go about with a certain Dominican, who is regarded as a holy man. For my part I do not believe it, for he often takes a cup of chocolate and immediately afterwards a good glass of strong Spanish wine; and I myself have had the honour of lunching with this saint who at table drank a whole decanter and finished up with a full glass of strong wine, two large slices of melon, some peaches, pears, five cups of coffee, a whole plate of cloves, and two full saucers of milk and lemon. He may of course be following some sort of diet, but I do not think so, for it would be too much; moreover he takes several little snacks during the afternoon. Addio. Farewell. Kiss Mamma's hands for me. My greetings to all who know me.

Wolfgang Mozart.

MOZART TO THOMAS LINLEY (AT FLORENCE)

Bologna
10 September 1770

My dear friend

Here is a letter at last! Indeed I am very late in replying to your charming letter addressed to me at Naples, which, however, I only received two months after you had written it. My father's plan was to travel to Loreto via Bologna, and thence to Milan via Florence, Leghorn and Genoa. We should by then have given you a surprise by turning up unexpectedly in Florence. But, as he had the misfortune to gash his leg rather badly when the shaft-horse of our sedia fell on the road, and as this wound not only kept him in bed for three weeks, but held us up in Bologna for another seven, this nasty accident has forced us to change our plans and to proceed to Milan via Parma.

Firstly, we have missed the suitable time for such a journey and, secondly, the season is over, as everyone is in the country and therefore we could not earn our expenses. I assure you that this accident has annoyed us very much. I would do everything in my power to have the pleasure of embracing my dear friend. Moreover my father and I would very much like to meet again Signor Gavard and his very dear and charming family, and also Signora Corilla and Signor Nardini, and then to return to Bologna. This we would do indeed, if we had the slightest hope of making even the expenses of our journey.

As for the engravings you lost, my father remembered you; and his order arrived in time for two other copies to be kept for you. So please let me know of some means of sending them to you. Keep me in your friendship and believe that my affection for you will endure for ever and that I am your most devoted servant and loving friend

Amadeo Wolfgang Mozart

In the following letter, Mozart is no longer the fashionable child prodigy but is faced with having to earn a living. The fact that he was essentially reliant on wealthy patrons is constantly recorded in his letters.

MOZART TO PADRE MARTINI (AT BOLOGNA)

Salzburg

4 September 1776

Most reverend Padre Maestro, my esteemed Patron,

The regard, the esteem and the respect which I cherish for your illustrious person have prompted me to trouble you with this letter and to send you a humble specimen of my music, which I submit to your masterly judgement. I composed for last year's carnival at Munich an opera buffa, ' La finta giardiniera'. A few days before my departure the Elector expressed a desire to hear some of my contrapuntal compositions. I was therefore obliged to write this motet in a great hurry, in order to have time to have the score copied for His Highness and to have the parts written out and thus enable it to be performed during the Offertory at High Mass on the following Sunday. Most beloved and esteemed Signor Padre Maestro! I beg you most earnestly to tell me, frankly and without reserve, what you think of it. We live in this world in order to learn zealously and, by interchanging our ideas, to enlighten one another and thus endeavour to promote science and art. Oh, how often have I longed to be near you, most Reverend Father, so that I might be able to talk and reason with you. For I live in a country where music leads a struggling existence, though indeed apart from those who have left us, we still have excellent teachers and particularly composers of great wisdom, learning and taste. As for the theatre, we are in a bad way for lack of singers. We have no castrati, and we shall never have them, as they insist on being handsomely paid, and generosity is not one of our faults. Meanwhile I am amusing myself by writing chamber music and music for the church, in which branches of composition we have two other excellent masters of counterpoint, Signori Haydn and Adlgasser. My father is in the service of the Cathedral and this gives me an opportunity of writing as much church music as I like. He has already served this court for thirty-six years and as he knows that the present Archbishop cannot and will not have anything to do with people who are getting on in years, he no longer puts his whole heart into his work, but has taken up literature, which was always a favourite study of his. Our church music is very different from that of Italy, since a Mass with the whole of the Kyrie, the Gloria, the Credo, the Epistle sonata, the Offertory or Motet, the Sanctus and the Agnus Dei must not last longer than three-quarters of an hour. This applies even to the most solemn Mass said by the Archbishop himself. So you see that a special study is required for this kind of composition. At the same time, the Mass must have all the instruments – trumpets, drums and so forth. Alas, that we are so far apart, my very dear Signor Padre Maestro! If we were together, I should have so many things to tell you! I send my devoted remembrances to all the members of the Accademia Filarmonica. I long to win your favour and I never cease to grieve that I am far away from that one person in the world whom I love, revere and esteem most of all and whose most humble and devoted servant, most

Reverend Father, I shall always be.

Wolfgang Amadeus Mozart.

From 1769 the Archbishop of Salzburg had taken a benevolent interest in Leopold's son but by 1777, desperate for funds, Mozart applied for leave of absence from his service. As a result of this petition both Mozart and his father were told that they had the Archbishop's permission to be released, though, in the event, Leopold stayed on and Mozart went off to Munich, accompanied by his mother.

Salzburg,
1 August 1777

Your Grace, Most Worthy Prince of the Holy Roman Empire!

I will not presume to trouble Your Grace with a full description of our unhappy circumstances, which my father has set forth most accurately in his very humble petition which was handed to you on March 14th, 1777. As, however, your most gracious decision was never conveyed to him, my father intended last June once more most respectfully to beg Your Grace to allow us to travel for a few months in order to enable us to make some money; and he would have done so, if you had not given orders that in view of the imminent visit of His Majesty the Emperor your orchestra should practise various works with a view to their performance. Later my father again applied for leave of absence, which Your Grace refused to grant, though you permitted me, who am in any case only a half-time servant, to travel alone. Our situation is pressing and my father has therefore decided to let me go alone. But to this course also Your Grace has been pleased to raise certain objections. Most Gracious Prince and Lord! Parents endeavour to place their children in a position to earn their own bread; and in this they follow alike their own interest and that of the State. The greater the talents which children have received from God, the more are they bound to use them for the improvement of their own and their parents' circumstances, so that they may at the same time assist them and take thought for their own future progress. The Gospel teaches us to use our talents in this way. My conscience tells me that I owe it to God to be grateful to my father, who has spent his time unwearyingly upon my education, so that I may lighten his burden, look after myself and later on be able to support my sister. For I should be sorry to think that she should have spent so many hours at the harpsichord and not be able to make good use of her training.

Your Grace will therefore be so good as to allow me to ask you most humbly for my discharge, of which I should like to take advantage before the autumn, so that I may not be obliged to face the bad weather of the ensuing months of winter. Your Grace will not misunderstand this petition, seeing that when I asked you for permission to travel to Vienna three years ago, you graciously declared that I had nothing to hope for in Salzburg and would do better to seek my fortune elsewhere. I thank Your Grace for all the favours I have received from you and, in the hope of being able to serve you later on with greater success, I am

your most humble and obedient servant
Wolfgang Amadé Mozart

Mozart was successful and happy in Munich but he missed his father and wrote to him regularly. 'We are living like princes. Only one person is wanting – and that is Papa.'

Almost as soon as Mozart arrived in Munich it was arranged that he should have the opportunity to meet the Elector. In a letter to his father he describes the meeting:

When the Elector came up to me, I said: 'Your Highness will allow me to throw myself most humbly at your feet and offer you my services.' 'So you have left Salzburg for good?' 'Yes, your Highness, for good.' 'How is that? Have you had a row with him?' 'Not at all, your Highness. I only asked him for permission to travel, which he refused. So I was compelled to take this step, though indeed I had long been intending to clear out. For Salzburg is no place for me, I can assure you.' 'Good Heavens! There's a young man for you! But your father is still in Salzburg?' 'Yes your Highness. He too throws himself most humbly at your feet, and so forth. I have been three times to Italy already, I have written three operas, I am a member of the Bologna Academy, where I had to pass a test, at which many maestri have laboured and sweated for four or five hours, but which I finished in an hour. Let that be a proof that I am competent to serve at any court. My sole wish, however, is to serve your Highness, who himself is such a great – ' 'Yes, my dear boy, but I have no vacancy. I am sorry. If only there were a vacancy – ' 'I assure your Highness that I should not fail to do credit to Munich.' 'I know. But it is no good, for there is no vacancy here.' This he said as he walked away. Whereupon I commended myself to his good graces...

From Germany Mozart travelled to Paris. Still short of money, he says in a letter to his father: 'I have now set all my hopes on Paris, for the German princes are all skinflints.'

Things immediately started to improve and he very quickly received commissions, the *Concerto for flute and harp, K.299* being one. He was also engaged by the Duc de Guines to teach his daughter composition.

The following fragment of a letter to his father shows what a thoughtful and committed teacher Mozart could be.

Paris,
14 May 1778

I have so much to do already, that I wonder what it will be like in winter! I think I told you in my last letter that the Duc de Guines, whose daughter is my pupil in composition, plays the flute extremely well, and that she plays the harp *magnifique*. She has a great deal of talent, even genius, and in particular a marvellous memory, so that she can play all her pieces, actually about two hundred, by heart. She is, however, extremely doubtful as to whether she has any talent for composition, especially as regards invention or ideas. But her father who, between ourselves, is somewhat too infatuated with her, declares that she certainly has ideas and that it is only that she is too bashful and has too little self-confidence. Well, we shall see. If she gets no inspirations or ideas (for at present she really has none whatever), then it is to no purpose, for – God knows – I can't give her any. Her father's intention is not to make a great composer of her. 'She is not', he said, 'to compose operas, arias, concertos, symphonies, but only grand sonatas for her instrument and mine.' I gave her her fourth lesson today and, so far as the rules of composition and harmony are concerned, I am fairly well satisfied with her. She filled in quite a good bass for the first minuet, the melody of which I had given her, and she has already begun to write in three parts. But she very soon gets bored, and I am unable to help her; for as yet I cannot proceed more quickly. It is too soon, even if there really were genius there, but unfortunately there is none. Everything has to be done by rule. She has no ideas whatever – nothing comes. I have tried her in every possible way Among other things I hit on the idea of writing down a very simple minuet, in order to see whether she could not compose a variation on it. It was useless. 'Well,' I thought, 'she probably does not know how she ought to begin.' So I started to write a variation on the first bar and told her to go on in the same way and to keep to the idea. In the end it went fairly well. When it was finished, I told her to begin something of her own, – only the treble part, the melody. Well, she thought and thought for a whole quarter of an hour and nothing came. So I wrote down four bars of a minuet and said to her: 'See what an ass I am! I have begun a minuet and cannot even finish the melody. Please be so kind as to finish it for me.' She was positive she couldn't, but at last with great difficulty – something came, and indeed I was only too glad to see something for once. I then told her to finish the minuet, I mean, the treble only. But for home work all I asked her to do was to alter my four bars and compose something of her own. She was to find a new beginning, use, if necessary, the same harmony, provided that the melody should be different. Well, I shall see tomorrow what she has done…

> Whilst in Paris Mozart's mother died. Soon after, he went back to his
> beloved Mannheim and then to Munich. It was there that he prepared
> for the production of his first great opera *Idomeneo*. Since the librettist,
> the Abbate Giambattista Varesco, was the court chaplain in Salzburg,
> Mozart used his father as intermediary.

Munich,
8 November 1780

Mon très cher Père!

…I have just one request to make of the Abbate. Ilia's aria in Act II, Scene 2, should be altered slightly to suit what I require. 'Se il padre perdei, in te lo ritrovo'; this verse could not be better. But now comes what has always seemed unnatural to me – I mean, in an aria – and that is, a spoken aside. In a dialogue all these things are quite natural, for a few words can be spoken aside hurriedly; but in an aria where the words have to be repeated, it has a bad effect, and even if this were not the case, I should prefer an uninterrupted aria. The beginning may stand, if it suits him, for the poem is charming and, as it is absolutely natural and flowing and therefore as I have not got to contend with difficulties arising from the words, I can go on composing quite easily; for we have agreed to introduce here an aria *andantino* with obbligatos for four wind-instruments, that is, a flute, oboe, horn and bassoon…

Munich,
15 November 1780

… The aria is excellent now, but there is still one more alteration, for which Raaff is responsible. He is right, however, – and even if he were not, some courtesy ought to be shown to his grey hairs. He was with me yesterday. I ran through his first aria for him and he was well pleased with it. Well – the man is old and can no longer show off in such an aria as that in Act II – 'Fuor del mar ho un mar nel seno'. So, as he has no aria in Act III and as his aria in Act I, owing to the expression of the words, cannot be as *cantabile* as he would like, he wishes to have a pretty one to sing (instead of the quartet) after his last speech, 'O Creta fortunata! O me felice!' Thus a useless piece will be got rid of – and Act III will be far more effective. In the last scene of Act II Idomeneo has an aria or rather a sort of cavatina between the choruses. Here it will be better to have a mere recitative, well supported by the instruments. For in this scene which will be the finest in the whole opera (on account of the action and grouping which were settled recently with Le Grand), there will be so much noise and confusion on the stage that an aria at this particular point would cut a poor figure – and moreover there is the thunderstorm, which is not likely to subside during Herr Raaff's aria, is it? The effect, therefore, of a recitative between the choruses will be infinitely better…

Munich,
29 November 1780

…Tell me, don't you think that the speech of the subterranean voice is too long? Consider it carefully. Picture to yourself the theatre, and remember that the voice must be terrifying – must penetrate – that the audience must believe that it really exists. Well, how can this effect be produced if the speech is too long, for in this case the listeners will become more and more convinced that it means nothing. If the speech of the Ghost in 'Hamlet' were not so long, it would be far more effective. It is easy to shorten the speech of the subterranean voice and it will gain thereby more than it will lose.

For the march in Act II, which is heard in the distance, I require mutes for the trumpets and horns, which it is impossible to get here. Will you send me one of each by the next mail coach, so that I may have them copied?

Munich,
19 December 1780

…The scene between father and son in Act I and the first scene in Act II between Idomeneo and Arbace are both too long. They would certainly bore the audience, particularly as in the first scene both the actors are bad, and in the second, one of them is; besides, they only contain a narrative of what the spectators have already seen with their own eyes. These scenes are being printed as they stand. But I should like the Abbate to indicate how they may be shortened – and as drastically as possible, – for otherwise I shall have to shorten them myself. These two scenes cannot remain as they are – I mean, when set to music...

Munich,
3 January 1781

Mon très cher Père!

My head and my hands are so full of Act III that it would be no wonder if I were to turn into a third act myself. This act alone has cost me more trouble than the whole opera, for there is hardly a scene in it which is not extremely interesting. The accompaniment to the subterranean voice consists of five instruments only, that is, three trombones and two French horns, which are placed in the same quarter as that from which the voice proceeds. At this point the whole orchestra is silent...

No doubt we shall have a good many points to raise in Act III, when it is staged. For example, in Scene 6, after Arbace's aria, I see that Varesco has Idomeneo, Arbace, etc. How can the latter reappear immediately? Fortunately he can stay away altogether. But for safety's sake I have composed a somewhat longer introduction to the High Priest's recitative. After the mourning chorus the king and all his people go away; and in the following scene the directions are, '*Idomeneo in ginocchione nel tempio*'. That is quite impossible. He must come in with his whole suite. A march must be introduced here, and I have therefore composed a very simple one for two violins, viola, cello and two oboes, to be played a *mezza voce*. While it is going on The King appears and the priests prepare the offerings for the sacrifice. The King then kneels down and begins the prayer.

In Elettra's recitative, after the subterranean voice has spoken, there ought to be an indication – *Partono*. I forgot to look at the copy which has been made for the printer to see whether there is one, and if so, where it comes. It seems to me very silly that they should hurry away so quickly for no better reason than to allow Madame Elettra to be alone.

Always the servant rather than the freelance artist he would have liked to have been, Mozart was then commanded by the Archbishop to go to Vienna. He had finished *Idomeneo* whilst in Munich. In 1782 he married Constanze Weber, the third daughter of Mme Weber, his landlady.

It is always interesting to hear of one composer's opinion of another. In one letter Mozart describes Clementi as a 'mere mechanic' after a keyboard 'duel' between the two of them. In the following letter Mozart offers a harsh and perhaps unfair opinion of Clementi. He included these views with news of his wife's forthcoming confinement.

Vienna,
7 June 1783

Mon très cher Père!

Praise and thanks be to God, I am quite well again! But my illness has left me a cold as a remembrance, which was very charming of it! I have received my dear sister's letter. My wife's name-day is neither in March nor in May, but on February 16th; and is not to be found in any calendar. She thanks you both, however, most cordially, for your kind good wishes, which are always acceptable, even though it is not her name-day. She wanted to write to my sister herself, but in her present condition she must be excused if she is a little bit *commode* – or, as we say, indolent. According to the midwife's examination she ought to have had her confinement on the 4th, but I do not think that the event will take place before the 15th or 16th. She is longing for it to happen as soon as possible, particularly that she may have the happiness of embracing you and my dear sister in Salzburg. As I did not think that this would happen so soon, I kept on postponing going down on my knees, folding my hands and entreating you most submissively, my dearest father, to be godfather! As there is still time, I am doing so now. Meanwhile (in the confident hope that you will not refuse) I have already arranged (I mean, since the midwife took stock of the *visum repertum*) that someone shall present the child in your name, whether it is *generis masculini* or *feminini!* So we are going to call it Leopold or Leopoldine.

Well, I have a few words to say to my sister about Clementi's sonatas. Everyone who either hears them or plays them must feel that as compositions they are worthless. They contain no remarkable or striking passages except those in sixths and octaves. And I implore my sister not to practise those passages too much, so that she may not spoil her quiet, even touch and that her hand may not lose its natural lightness, flexibility and smooth rapidity. For after all what is to be gained by it? Supposing that you do play sixths and octaves with the utmost velocity (which no one can accomplish, not even Clementi) you only produce an atrocious chopping effect and nothing else whatever. Clementi is a *ciarlatano*, like all Italians. He writes *Presto* over a sonata or even *Prestissimo* and *Alla breve*, and plays it himself *Allegro* in 4/4 time. I know this is the case, for I have heard him do so. What he really does well are his passages in thirds; but he sweated over them day and night in London. Apart from this, he can do nothing, absolutely nothing, for he has not the slightest expression or taste, still less, feeling...

> Mozart was by now in close touch with Haydn and often joined him, when he was in Vienna, to play string quartets at Prince Esterhazy's private concerts. Mozart took the viola part. He dedicated a set of six Quartets to Haydn,.calling them his six sons. The second of these, the *Quartet in D minor*, was written whilst his wife, Constanze, was giving birth to their first child in the next room. The baby was eagerly awaited but Mozart could always separate his personal concerns from his extraordinary creative drive.

MOZART TO JOSEPH HAYDN (AT EISENSTADT)

Vienna,
1 September 1785

To my dear friend Haydn

A father who had decided to send out his sons into the great world, thought it his duty to entrust them to the protection and guidance of a man who was very celebrated at the time and who, moreover, happened to be his best friend.

In like manner I send my six sons to you, most celebrated and very dear friend. They are, indeed, the fruit of a long and laborious study; but the hope which many friends have given me that this toil will be in some degree rewarded, encourages me and flatters me with the thought that these children may one day prove a source of consolation to me.

During your last stay in this capital you yourself, my very dear friend, expressed to me your approval of these compositions. Your good opinion encourages me to offer them to you and leads me to hope that you will not consider them wholly unworthy of your favour. Please then receive them kindly and be to them a father, guide and friend! From this moment I surrender to you all my rights over them. I entreat you, however, to be indulgent to those faults which may have escaped a father's partial eye, and, in spite of them, to continue your generous friendship towards one who so highly appreciates it. Meanwhile, I remain with all my heart, dearest friend, your most sincere friend.

W. A. Mozart

Although this was the most fertile period of Mozart's life during which he composed *The Marriage of Figaro, Don Giovanni* and his last three great symphonies, he was, nevertheless, besieged by money problems. One of the people to whom he turned was Michael Puchberg, a rich merchant and a fellow freemason. B.O. stands for Brother of the Order.

MOZART TO MICHAEL PUCHBERG

Vienna,
early July 1788

Dearest Friend and B.O.

Owing to great difficulties and complications my affairs have become so involved that it is of the utmost importance to raise some money on these two pawnbroker's tickets. In the name of our friendship I implore you to do me this favour; but you must do it immediately. Forgive my importunity, but you know my situation. Ah! If only you had done what I asked you! Do it even now – then everything will be as I desire.

Ever your
Mozart

Constanze and Mozart were apart a great deal because of Mozart's engagements and he wrote lively and loving letters from all over Germany:

MOZART TO CONSTANZE

Berlin,
19 May 1789

Dearest, most beloved little Wife of my Heart

Well, I trust that you will by now have received some letters from me, for they can't all have been lost. This time I can't write very much to you, as I have to pay some calls and I am only sending you this to announce my arrival.

I shall probably be able to leave by the 25th; at least I shall do my best to do so. But I shall let you know definitely before then. I shall quite certainly get away by the 27th. Oh, how glad I shall be to be with you again, my darling! But the first thing I shall do is to take you by your front curls; for how on earth could you think, or even imagine, that I had forgotten you? How could I possibly do so? For even supposing such a thing you will get on the very first night a thorough spanking... and this you may count upon.

Adieu.

Ever your only friend and your husband

who loves you with all his heart

W.A. Mozart

LUDWIG VAN BEETHOVEN
1770–1827

Beethoven was born in Bonn the son of a singer in the service of the Elector of Cologne. At seventeen, whilst by now also in the service of the Elector, he was sent on a short visit to Vienna, where he took lessons from Mozart. Five years later, Beethoven quitted the service of the Elector of Cologne and moved to Vienna, initially studying with Haydn. Beethoven stayed in Vienna for the rest of his life making an independent living as composer and performer. He worked during a period of transition; composers were moving away from being solely in the employ of the nobility and were more free to take on other commissions and fees. He was able to take advantage of both. Although he was dependent on patronage early in his career in Bonn, by the age of thirty he was so successful from commissions and fees from publishers that he was able to continue receiving financial support from rich patrons, without loss of personal and artistic independence. Indeed, when the King of Westfalia tried to poach Beethoven in 1808, three of his most aristocratic patrons combined to pay him a substantial annual pension to remain in Vienna.

Beethoven's letters reflect his character – passionate, moody, short tempered and sometimes rude or even offensive, and are written with a wonderful lack of restraint. These two letters to an old and respected friend show his ability to flare up, only to regret it, immediately.

Vienna, 1799

Never come near me again! you are a faithless cur, and may the hangman take all faithless curs.

Beethoven

My dearest Nazerl,
You are an honest fellow and I now perceive you were right; so come to see me this afternoon; Schuppanzigh will be here too, and the pair of us will scold you, cuff you and shake you to your heart's content.

A warm embrace from
your Beethoven
also known as Little Dumpling

By the age of thirty, Beethoven was already one of the outstanding composers of the day. He was also famous as a virtuoso pianist and was patronised generously by Viennese aristocracy. However, also at this time, his deafness had become apparent to him, and in this letter to his friend Carl Amenda, he poignantly admits to its presence but swears him to secrecy.

Vienna,
July 1, 1801

...How often would I like to have you here with me, for your B[eethoven] is leading a very unhappy life and is at variance with Nature and his Creator. Many times already I have cursed Him for exposing His creatures to the slightest hazard, so that the most beautiful blossom is thereby often crushed and destroyed. Let me tell you that my most prized possession, *my hearing*, has greatly deteriorated. When you were still with me, I already felt the symptoms; but I said nothing about them. Now they have become much worse. We must wait and see whether my hearing can be restored. The symptoms are said to be caused by the condition of my abdomen. So far as the latter is concerned, I am almost cured. But that my hearing too will improve, I must hope, it is true, but I hardly think it possible, for diseases of that kind are the most difficult to cure. You will realise what a sad life I must now lead, seeing that I am cut off from everything that is dear and precious to me and, what is more, have to associate with such miserable egotists as Zmeskall, Schuppanzigh and the like...

Oh, how happy should I be now if I had perfect hearing, for then I would join you immediately. But in my present condition I must withdraw from everything; and the best years will rapidly pass away without my being able to achieve all that my talent and my strength have commanded me to do – Sad resignation, to which I am forced to have recourse. Needless to say, I am resolved to overcome all this, but how is it to be done?...

I beg you to treat what I have told you about my hearing as a great secret to be entrusted to no one, whoever he may be – Write to me very often, for your letters, however short they may be, console me and do me good...

Well, best wishes, my dear good fellow. If you know of anything perhaps that I can do for you here to give you pleasure, you understand, of course, that you must inform first of all

your faithful, your truly devoted
L.v. Beethoven

In this letter Beethoven vents his frustration on his publishers for the capricious responses of their reviewers to his music.

BEETHOVEN TO BREITKOPF & HARTEL, PUBLISHERS.

Vienna,
22 April 1801

...Advise your reviewers to be more circumspect and intelligent, particularly in regard to the productions of younger composers. For many a one, who perhaps might go far, may take fright. As for myself, far be it from me to think that I have achieved a perfection which suffers no adverse criticism. But your reviewer's outcry against me was at first very mortifying. Yet when I began to compare myself with other composers, I could hardly bring myself to pay any attention to it but remained quite calm and said to myself: 'They don't know anything about music'. And indeed what made it easier for me to keep calm was that I noticed how certain people were being praised to the skies who in

Vienna had very little standing among the best local composers – practically none at all, whatever other excellent qualities they might possess – However, pax vobiscum – Peace between you and me – I should never have mentioned a syllable of all this, if you yourself had not raised the point –

> Ten years later and Beethoven's opinion of publisher's reviewers has not improved.

BEETHOVEN TO BREITKOPF & HARTEL

Vienna,
9 October 1811

...Arrange for the oratorio, and in general everything else, to be reviewed by whomever you like. I am sorry that I wrote a single word to you about those wretched reviewers. Who would bother his head about reviewers of that type when he sees how just such wretched reviewers extol the most contemptible bunglers and how, on the whole, they deal with works of art in the most insulting manner and, admittedly, are bound to do so, seeing that they are so clumsy, and, unlike the cobbler with his last, fail to discover and apply at once the appropriate standard of excellence...

Well, you may go on reviewing as long as you like; and I wish you much enjoyment. Even if the composer feels something like a gnat biting him, well the pain is soon gone; and when the engraving has been done, there is something really pleasant to enjoy. You *can't* go on re-re-re-re-re-vi-vi-ew-ew-ing-ing-ing *to all eternity, that you can't do.* So now God be with you...

> Beethoven greatly admired Goethe, some twenty years his senior. When they eventually met in the Bohemian health resort of Terplitz in 1812 there was a certain amount of mutual disappointment. Goethe was by now a Cabinet Minister to a Sovereign Prince whilst Beethoven retained his republican opinions.

BEETHOVEN TO BREITKOPF AND HARTEL

Franzensbrunn, near Egar,
August 9, 1812

... Goethe delights far too much in the court atmosphere, far more than is becoming in a poet. How can one really say very much about the ridiculous behaviour of virtuosi in this respect, when poets, who should be regarded as the leading teachers of the nation, can forget everything else when confronted with that glitter –

Your
Beethoven

GOETHE TO FRIEDRICH ZELTER

Karlsbad,
2 September 1812

...I made Beethoven's acquaintance at Terplitz. His talent amazed me; but unfortunately he is a completely untamed personality, who indeed is not mistaken in finding the world detestable, but who certainly does not make it more enjoyable, either for himself or for other people, by saying so. But he is much to be excused, and much to be pitied because he is losing his hearing – which is perhaps less damaging to the musical side of his being than to the social side. He is of a laconic disposition anyway, and this defect makes him doubly so...

> Within a few years the only way of communicating with Beethoven was to write in a conversation book.
> A very different Beethoven from the crusty writer of the previous letters is seen in this trio of love letters to an unknown woman. They were found in a secret drawer in his desk immediately after his death during a search for some bank shares bequeathed by Beethoven to his nephew. Despite much research and speculation by numerous scholars and biographers, the identity of the recipient of these letters remains a mystery and it seems unlikely that they were ever sent.

BEETHOVEN TO AN UNKNOWN WOMAN

Terplitz,
July 6 and 7 1812

July 6th, in the morning

My angel, my all, my very self. – Only a few words today, and, what is more, written in pencil (and with your pencil) – I shan't be certain of my rooms here until tomorrow; what an unnecessary waste of time is all this – Why this profound sorrow, when necessity speaks – can our love endure without sacrifices, without our demanding everything from one another; can you alter the fact that you are not wholly mine, and that I am not wholly yours? – Dear God, look at Nature in all her beauty and set your heart at rest about what must be – Love demands all, and rightly so, and thus it is *for me with you, for you with me* – But you forget so easily that I must live *for me and for you*; if we were completely united, you would feel this painful necessity just as little as I do – My journey was dreadful and I did not arrive here until yesterday at four o'clock in the morning. As there were few horses the mail coach chose another route, but what a dreadful road it was; at the last stage but one I was warned not to travel at night; attempts were made to frighten me about a forest, but all this spurred me on to proceed – and it was wrong of me to do so. The coach broke down, of course, owing to the dreadful road which had not been made up and was nothing but a country track. If I hadn't had those two postilions I should have been left stranded on the way – On the other ordinary road Esterházy with eight horses met with the same fate as I did with four – Yet I felt to a certain extent the pleasure I always feel when I have overcome some difficulty successfully – Well, let me turn quickly from outer to inner experiences. No doubt we shall meet soon; and today also time fails me to tell you of the thoughts which during these last few days I have been revolving about my life – If our hearts were always so closely united, I would certainly entertain no such thoughts. My heart overflows with a longing to tell you so many things – Oh – there are moments when I find that speech is quite inadequate – Be cheerful – and be for ever my faithful, my only sweetheart, my all, as I am yours. The gods must send us everything else, whatever must and shall be our fate –

Your faithful
Ludwig

Monday evening,
July 6th

You are suffering, you, my most precious one – I have noticed this very moment that letters have to be handed in very early, on Monday – or on Thursday – the only days when the mail coach goes from here to K. – You are suffering – Oh, where I am, you are with me – I will see to it that you and I, that I can live with you. What a life!!! as it is now!!!! without you – pursued by the kindness of people here and there, a kindness that I think – that I wish to deserve just as little as I deserve it – man's homage to man – that pains me –

and when I consider myself in the setting of the universe, what am I and what is that man – whom one calls the greatest of men – and yet – on the other hand therein lies the divine element in man – I weep when I think that probably you will not receive the first news of me until Saturday – However much you love me – my love for you is even greater – but never conceal yourself from me – good night – Since I am taking the baths I must get off to sleep – Dear God – so near! so far! Is not our love truly founded in heaven – and, what is more, as strongly cemented as the firmament of Heaven?

Good morning, on July 7th
Even when I am in bed my thoughts rush to you, my eternally beloved, now and then joyfully, then again sadly, waiting to know whether Fate will hear our prayer – To face life I must live altogether with you or never see you. Yes, I am resolved to be a wanderer abroad until I can fly to your arms and say that I have found my true home with you and enfolded in your arms can let my soul be wafted to the realm of blessed spirits – alas, unfortunately it must be so – You will become composed, the more so as you know that I am faithful to you; no other woman can ever possess my heart – never – never – Oh God, why must one be separated from her who is so dear. Yet my life in V at present is a miserable life – Your love has made me both the happiest and the unhappiest of mortals – At my age I now need stability and regularity in my life – can this coexist with our relationship? – Angel, I have just heard that the post goes every day – and therefore I must close, so that you receive the letter immediately – Be calm; for only by calmly considering our lives can we achieve our purpose to live together – Be calm – love me – Today – yesterday – what tearful longing for you – for you – you – my life – my all – all good wishes to you – Oh, do continue to love me – never misjudge your lover's most faithful heart.

ever yours
ever mine
ever ours

FRANZ SCHUBERT
1797–1828

Franz Schubert was born in Vienna and lived the whole of his short life there. On leaving the choir school of the Chapel Royal he helped in his father's school before giving up everything for music, living frugally, helped by generous friends.

Schubert never met Beethoven although they both lived in Vienna and Schubert was a great admirer. Just as the humble Schubert did not approach the mighty Beethoven, neither did he approach the important and powerful people who had patronized Beethoven. When he died Schubert was hardly known outside Vienna despite being the composer of a great volume of work, including symphonies, piano sonatas and chamber works, and being the greatest ever writer of Lieder.

As was so often the case with musicians, Schubert from a young age was habitually short of money. In this letter he is writing from his choir school.

SCHUBERT TO HIS BROTHER FERDINAND

Vienna

24 November 1812.

...I shall come straight out with what I have in mind, for this will bring me the sooner to my purpose and you will not be kept in suspense by my beating about the bush. For a long time I have been thinking over my circumstances, and have concluded that while on the whole they are good, yet in certain respects they might be better. You know by experience that now and then a fellow has a fancy to eat a roll of bread and an apple or two – especially when he has not had much of a midday dinner and can only look forward to a scanty supper 8 and a half hours later. This desire, which I have often felt keenly, is becoming more and more importunate, and willy-nilly I must find some way of changing the situation. My beggarly allowance from our respected father is scattered to the winds in the first few days, and what am I to do for the rest of the time? "They who put their trust in thee shall not perish" (St Matthew, Chap. 3 v.4). And I think so too. How would it be if you were to send me a few shillings a month? You would not even feel it, for then I should think myself happy in my retreat and be satisfied. As I said before, I base myself on the words of the Apostle Matthew, who also says "He that has two cloaks, let

57

him give one to the poor", etc. Meanwhile, I hope you will listen to the voice, which is ceaselessly calling on you,

of your

affectionate, impoverished, hopeful

and – I repeat – impoverished brother

Franz

In 1818 Schubert was employed by Count Johann Esterhazy (a distant relative of Haydn's Esterhazys) to give piano lessons to his daughters. He was shocked to find that, in the country, on the Count's estate, he was lodged in the servants' quarters, taking meals with the staff. He longed for letters.

SCHUBERT TO HIS BROTHER

Zseliz,

29 October 1818

Dear brother Ferdinand,

For the sin of your appropriation I had already forgiven you in my first letter. So your long delay in writing can have no other reason than, perhaps, your tender conscience. You liked the funeral mass, it made you weep, and perhaps at the same point where I myself wept; dear brother, that is my greatest reward for the gift, you need not mention any other.

If only I were not getting to know the people around me better every day, I should be contented here as I was at first. But now I perceive that I am really alone among them all, except for a couple of genuinely good-natured girls...

The local parson, who is a big old so-and-so, as stupid as an arch-ass and as coarse as a buffalo, preaches sermons that put the much revered Pater Nepomucene into the shade. It is a joy to listen to him hurling epithets such as 'carrion', 'canaille', etc., from the pulpit, or bringing out a skull and saying 'Take a look at this, you cross-eyed dullards, that's what you will all look like one day', or 'Yes, a lad goes with his hussy to the tavern, dances all night, then they go tipsy to bed and when they get up there are three of them', etc.

Schubert was to return to Vienna later that year. In 1823 he contracted syphilis.

SCHUBERT TO SCHOBER

Steyr,
14th August 1823

Dear Schober:

Although I write rather late, I hope that this letter will still find you in Vienna. I correspond busily with Schäffer and I am fairly well. Whether I shall ever quite recover I am inclined to doubt. Here I live very simply in every respect, go for walks regularly, work much at my opera and read Walter Scott.

With Vogl I get on very well. We are at Linz together, where he sang a good deal, and splendidly. Bruchmann, Sturm and Streinsberg came to see us at Steyr a few days ago, and they too were dismissed with a full load of songs.

As I shall hardly see you before your return, I once again wish you the best of good fortune in your enterprise and assure you of my everlasting affection, which will make me miss you most sorely. Wherever you may be give news of yourself from time to time to

Your friend
Franz Schubert.

In 1827 Schubert accepted an invitation from Marie Koschako to visit Gratz. She was a pianist who was married to a lawyer, Dr Karl Pachler. Their house became a centre for the social and musical life of Gratz. Marie greatly admired Beethoven and when in 1817 they met, a friendship developed and Beethoven became very fond of Marie. In fact Schindler even claimed her as a candidate for the 'Immortal Beloved'. Schubert's works were introduced to Gratz via its Music Society and Marie came to admire his work. She invited him to Gratz several times and in 1827 he accepted.

SCHUBERT TO MARIE PACHLER

Vienna,
12th June 1827

Madam,

Although I cannot imagine in what way I have deserved so kind an offer as your honour has informed me of by the letter sent to Jenger, nor whether I shall ever be able to offer anything in return, I nevertheless cannot forbear to accept an invitation whereby I shall not only set eyes at last on much-vaunted Gratz, but have the privilege, moreover, of making your honour's acquaintance.

I remain, with all respect
your honour's most devoted Frz. Schubert

He arrived on September 3rd with his friend Johann Jenger, who was also secretary to the Gratz Music Society, and stayed for three weeks. There he gave a concert which was so successful that it had to be repeated. He enjoyed his stay enormously and on his return home he wrote to Marie. For the first time he was disappointed to be in his beloved Vienna.

SCHUBERT TO MARIE PACHLER

Vienna,
September 1827

Madam,

Already it becomes clear to me that I was only too happy at Gratz, and I cannot as yet get accustomed to Vienna. True, it is rather large, but then it is empty of cordiality, candour, genuine thought, reasonable words, and especially of intelligent deeds. There is so much confused chatter that one hardly knows whether one is on one's head or one's heels, and one rarely or never achieves inward contentment, 'Tis possible, of course, that the fault is largely my own, since I take a long time to warm up. At Gratz I soon recognised an artless and sincere way of being together, and a longer stay would have allowed me to take to it even more readily. Above all, I shall never forget the kindly shelter, where, with its dear hostess and the sturdy "Pachleros", as well as little Faust*, I spent the happiest days I have had for a long time. Hoping to be yet able to prove my gratitude in an adequate manner, I remain, with profound respect,

Most devotedly yours,
Frz. Schubert

*Faust is the Pachler's son, named in honour of Goethe.

Schubert's shortage of money was due in part to the difficulty of getting paid by publishers. This is illustrated in these letters to two of them, Schott and Probst.

SCHUBERT TO SCHOTT

Vienna,
October 2, 1828

Sirs:

As it is now such a long time since I had a letter from you, and I should be very glad to know whether you have received the composition I sent you, viz. 4 impromptus and the five-part male chorus, which I dispatched through Harlinger, I shall be glad if you would kindly let me have a reply on the subject. I am particularly anxious that the said composition should appear as soon as possible. The opus number for the Impromptus is 101 and that for the quintet 102. In anticipation of a speedy and agreeable reply.

With all respect,
Frz. Schubert

SCHUBERT TO PROBST

Vienna,
October 2, 1828

Sir:

I beg to inquire when the Trio is to appear at last. Can it be that you do not know the opus number yet? It is Op. 100. I await its appearance with longing. I have composed, among other things, 3 Sonatas for pianoforte, solo, which I should like to dedicate to Hummel. Moreover, I have set several songs by Heine of Hamburg, which pleased extraordinarily here, and finally turned out a Quintet for 2 violins, 1 viola, and 2 violoncellos.* The Sonatas I have played with much success in several places, but the Quintet will be tried out only during the coming days. If perchance any of these compositions would suit you, let me know.

With much respect,
I subscribe myself,
Frz. Schubert

*String Quintet in C Major.

61

They replied with various excuses for the delays, Schotts even complained that the Quintet was too short and offered 30 florins for it against the 60 previously agreed. Schubert did not accept this attempt to halve his modest fee.

Mainz,
30 October 1828

Herr Fr. Schubert in Vienna.

Your very much valued letters of 18th May and 2nd October have duly reached us. Our reply to the former was much delayed because we too waited for an opportunity to send the Impromptus from here to Paris, when they arrived here.

We have received them back from there with the intimation that these works are too difficult for trifles and would find no outlet in France, and we earnestly beg your pardon for this.

The Quintet we shall publish soon; but we are bound to observe that this small opus is too dear at the fee fixed, for the whole occupies but six printed pages in the pianoforte part, and we assume that it is by some error that we are asked to pay 60 fl., A.C., for this.

We offer you 30 fl. for it, and shall at once settle this amount on hearing from you, or you may draw upon us.

The Pianoforte work, Op. 101, we certainly do not regard as too expensive, but its impracticality for France vexed us considerably. If at any time you should write something less difficult and yet brilliant in an easier key, please send it to us without more ado.

We remain, respectfully and in friendship,
B. Schott's Sons

Probst did eventually publish the Trio, but so late that Schubert never saw a copy. The three sonatas were not published until ten years after the composer's death when they were published by Diabelli and dedicated, not to Hummel, who had died, but to Schumann. The Heine songs were included in the *Swan Song* cycle. The *String Quintet in C major* was not performed until 1850 and not published for another three years.

The following is Schubert's last letter. He was only thirty-two years old when he died and was still correcting the second part of his song cycle *Die Winterreise*.

Like Berlioz, Schubert was fond of the tales of the wild west which were fashionable at the time.

Vienna,
12 November 1828

Dear Schober,

I am ill. For the last 11 days I have taken nothing to eat or drink; I can only totter feebly from my armchair to my bed and back. Rinna is treating me. If I do take any nourishment my body rejects it again at once.

In kindness, let me have some books to ease this desperate situation. Those of Cooper's I have read are *The Last of the Mohicans, The Spy, The Pilot* and *The Settlers*. If by any chance you have anything else by him, I do beseech you to leave for me with Frau v. Bogner at the coffee-house. My brother, who is the soul of conscientiousness, will bring it to me in the most conscientious manner. Or anything else instead.

Your friend
Schubert

HECTOR BERLIOZ
1803-1869

Berlioz was born near Grenoble, the son of a doctor. In 1821 he went to Paris to become a medical student. He had no wish to do this and later persuaded his family that he must follow his deep desire and become a composer. He was to become the greatest figure in the French Romantic movement. He was a holder of the prestigious 'Prix de Rome' and the composer of overtures, symphonies, a grand requiem and oratorio, as well as the operas *Benvenuto Cellini, Beatrice and Benedict* and the immense *The Trojans*.

Berlioz made frequent references to Mendelssohn whom he met in Italy in 1830. In spite of their widely divergent musical paths, their friendship seems to have been grounded in mutual respect. Yet in a letter to his mother Mendelssohn refers to Berlioz as 'a real grotesque, without a spark of talent.'

1843

My dear Berlioz

I thank you most warmly for your kind letter, and for still remembering our Rome friendship. For my part I shall never forget it so long as I live, and I am delighted that I shall soon be able to tell you so in person. It will be both a duty and a pleasure for me to do all I can to make your stay in Leipzig agreeable and profitable. I think I can promise you that you that you will be satisfied with the town – with the musicians and the public, that is. Before writing to you I consulted several people who know Leipzig better than I, and all agree with me that you should be able to give a first-rate concert. The expenses of orchestra, hall, advertising etc. will be 110 crowns; the receipts could be as much as 600 or 800. You should be here to arrange the programme and everything else that may be necessary a good ten days beforehand. In addition, the directors of the Subscription Concerts Society have instructed me to ask you whether you will agree to one of your works being performed at the concert to be held in aid of the poor of Leipzig on 22nd February – that is, after the concert which you will yourself have given. I hope you will accept this proposal. So, I recommend that you come here as soon as you are able to leave Weimar. I am delighted that I can shake you by the hand and say *willkommen* to Germany. Please don't laugh at my bad French, as you used to in Rome, and remain my friend, as you were then, as I shall always be yours.

Felix Mendelssohn-Bartholdy

In Leipzig, Berlioz performed some of Mendelssohn's works. At the time, Fenimore Cooper's Red Indian stories were popular and as a token of their friendship Berlioz suggested that they exchange batons. Mendelssohn sent him his slim, white stick but Berlioz sent Mendelssohn an enormous wooden cudgel with the following letter.

HECTOR BERLIOZ TO MENDELSSOHN

Leipzig,
February 1843

To Chief Mendelssohn,

Big Chief! We promised to exchange tomahawks. Here is mine, it is roughly made, yours is simple. Only squaws and pale-faces like ornate weapons. Be my brother, and when the Great Spirit sends us to the happy hunting-grounds, may our braves hang up our tomahawks side by side by the door where they meet to palaver.

Hector Berlioz

Berlioz's most ambitious work *Les Troyens* was only a brief success and disappeared from the opera repertory until the first full staging in the original French as a continuous performance at Covent Garden in 1969.

Berlioz was persuaded by a more diplomatic friend not to send this letter.

BERLIOZ TO THE EMPEROR

Paris,
28th March 1858

Sire,

I have just completed a grand opera, of which I have written the words and the music. Despite the boldness and variety of means employed, the resources available in Paris would be sufficient to perform it. Permit me, Sire, to read you the poem and then, if it should be so fortunate as to merit such a high honour, to crave your protection for the work. The Opéra is at present directed by an old friend of mine who professes the strangest views about my musical style – a style which he has never understood and which he is incapable of appreciating. The two conductors on his staff are mine enemies. Sire, defend me from my friend and as for my enemies, as the Italian proverb has it, I will defend myself. If having heard my poem, your Majesty does not judge it worthy of being produced, I shall sincerely and respectfully accept your decision. But I cannot submit my work to the approval of people whose judgement is obscured by prejudice and preconception, and whose opinions in consequence have no value for me. They would put forward the alleged inadequacy of the poem as a pretext for rejecting the music...Now let discouragement and disappointment come if they will: nothing can take away the fact that the work exists. It is grand and powerful and, for all the apparent complexity of means, quite straight-forward. Unhappily it is not vulgar, but that is a fault which Your Majesty will pardon; and the Paris public is beginning to realise that music has a higher purpose than the manufacture of agreeable sounds. Permit me therefore, Sire, to borrow the words one of the characters in the epic poem from which I have drawn my subject, and to say: *Arma citi properate viro* ['Quickly bring him his weapons!'], and I believe I shall take Latium.

I remain, Sire, with profoundest respect and devotion, Your Majesty's most humble and obedient servant.

Hector Berlioz
Member of the Institute

The opera was not to be performed again until the sixth of November 1863. The following letter is to his friend Richard Pohl, who translated his opera *Beatrice and Benedict* into German for the production in Weimar in 1862. He and his wife also acted as stand-in musicians when Berlioz needed them.

BERLIOZ TO RICHARD POHL

Paris,
7 November 1863

My dear Pohl,

The 2nd performance of *Les Troyens* was given yesterday and far surpassed even the brilliance of the first; it aroused feelings I shall not attempt to describe to you on the one hand, and rendered a few individuals inconceivably furious, I am told. Two of these maniacs heap me with insults this morning in the *Figaro* and the *Nain jaune*. Mme Charton is superb as Dido; you would probably not believe her capable of such lofty tragedy. The Septet was encored with tremendous applause, the love duet drew tears from a great part of the audience. It was an evening of embraces: a steady stream of musicians, men of letters, artists and critics came behind the scenes during the intervals to congratulate me. I had heard there would be a cabal, but it did not venture to declare itself. Apart from the two small newspapers I mentioned, all the rest express very warm approval. On Monday and on Sunday we shall see some more important papers...

FELIX MENDELSSOHN-BARTHOLDY
1809-1847

Mendelssohn was born in Hamburg, the son of a cultured and wealthy banker. His upbringing and education were sound and happy and his musical talent was recognized early. He was never to have to worry about making a living like so many other musicians. He was intellectually and musically gifted and his letters reveal an open, enthusiastic and engaging personality. He was close to his equally talented sister and indeed to his whole family.

When he was a boy he became a friend of Goethe and as a young man

his father sent him off to travel, believing this an important part of education. On these travels he met other distinguished people including
Wellington and Peel. The amount of travel and the variety of jobs he
undertook–such as conducting, performing and organising, in addition
to composing–were remarkable. He was a generous colleague being the
first to perform Schumann's symphonies, a good friend to Hector Berlioz
and a champion of many lesser known composers and performers.

MENDELSSOHN TO HIS FAMILY

London,
25 April 1829

...It is terrible! It is crazy! I am dazed and my head is spinning! London is
the grandest and most complicated monstrosity on the face of the earth. How
can I pack into a single letter all I have been through in the last three days? I
can scarcely remember the main points myself by now, but I must not keep a
diary, for that would cut down my experience further, and I don't want that – I
want to absorb everything that comes my way…But just step out of my lodging
and turn to the right down Regent Street, look at the splendid wide street
lined with porticos (unhappily, today again it is lying under a thick fog), and
look at the shops with their inscriptions, in letters as tall as a man, and the
stage-coaches piled high with passengers, and see how at one point a string of
conveyances is out-distanced by the pedestrians because it has been held up
by some elegant carriages, and how at another point a horse is rearing up
because its rider has acquaintances in yonder house, and how men are used to
carry round posters that promise us graceful and artistic performances by
trained cats – and the beggars and the negroes and the fat John Bulls with a
slim, pretty daughter on each arm. Oh, those daughters! But never fear, I run
no danger in that respect, either in Hyde Park, with its throng of ladies where
I took a fashionable stroll yesterday with Madame Moscheles, or at the
concert, or at the Opera (for I have been all over that already); the only
danger is at street-corners and crossings, where I often murmur to myself a
familiar phrase: 'Take care not to fall under the wheels!' Such confusion! Such
a maelstrom! I ask nothing better than to become historical and describe it all
calmly, else you will make nothing of it; but if you could only see me, sitting
near the heavenly grand piano that Clementi have just sent along for the
duration of my stay, beside a cheerful fire, within my own four walls, with my
shoes on, and my grey open-work stockings and my olive-green gloves (for I

have calls to pay presently), and next door my huge four-poster bed, in which I can 'lie down for a walk' at night, with the bright-coloured curtains and old-fashioned furniture, my breakfast tea and dry toast still in front of me, the *servant-girl*, with her hair in curl-papers, just bringing me my new cravat and asking for my orders – at which I try to nod in the polite English manner, jerking my head backwards – and the fashionable, fog-shrouded street; and if you could only hear the pitiful tones of the beggar who has just struck up a song under my window (but his voice is almost drowned by the cries of the hawkers), and if you but knew that from here to the *City* is a three-quarter-hour drive and that all the way along, and at every glimpse down the side streets and far into the distance one finds uproar, and that even so one has gone through only perhaps a quarter of populated London, you would understand that I am half out of my senses...

London,
15 May 1829

On Monday evening there was a ball at the Duke of Devonshire's; everything that wealth, luxury and taste could devise by way of beautiful touches for a ball, was assembled there...I had heard people coming up the steps behind me, but had not looked round, now I saw with a shock that it had been Wellington and Peel.

Weimar,
25 May 1830

...Goethe is so friendly and affable with me that I do not know how to thank him or to deserve it. This morning he made me play the piano to him for about an hour, pieces from all the great composers, in chronological order, and tell him how they had worked at them; while he sat in a dark corner, like *Jupiter tonans*, and his old eyes flashed lightning. He would have none of Beethoven. But I told him I could not help that, and thereupon played him the first movement of the C Minor Symphony. That affected him strangely. At first he said, 'But it does not move one at all; it merely astounds; it is grandiose', again; 'That is very great, quite mad, one is almost afraid the house will fall down; and only imagine when they are all playing together!'

Paris,
21 February 1832

...But it is now high time I wrote to you about my travel plans, my dear Father, and what I have to say this time will for many reasons be more serious than usual. First let me sum things up and speak of the aims you fixed for me before I went away, telling me to hold firmly to them. I was to take a close look at different countries, so as to find one where I should like to live and work; I was to make my name and abilities known, so that people would welcome me wherever I decided to settle, and sympathize with what I was trying to do; and finally, I was to make use of my good fortune and your kindness to lay the foundations of my future career. It makes me feel very happy to be able to tell you that I believe all this has been done. Apart from possible mistakes which one does not notice until too late, I think I have achieved the aims you set me. People already know I exist and want to do something, and they are sure to welcome anything good I may produce...Before I leave here (if it can be arranged), and certainly in London, if the cholera does not prevent me from going there in April, I intend to give a concert on my own and make a little money, which is something I also wanted to do before coming home to you; so I hope that this part of your plan – that I should make a name for myself – may be said to have been fulfilled. But your other intention, that I should find a country for myself, has also been met, at least in a general way. The country is Germany, I have now become quite convinced of that...

London,
11 May 1832

...I must tell you about an amusing morning I had last week. Of all the signs of recognition I have so far received, this was the one that pleased and touched me most, and perhaps the only one I shall always look back on with fresh delight. On Saturday morning the Philharmonic Orchestra was rehearsing, but they could not include anything by me because my Overture had not yet been copied out. After Beethoven's *Pastoral* Symphony, during which I was in a box, I went down into the hall to greet a few old friends. But I was scarcely down before someone in the orchestra called out 'There is

Mendelssohn', at which they all began to shout and clap so heartily that for a time I did not know which way to turn; and when that was over, someone else called out 'Welcome to him', and they began to make the same noise again, and I had to go right through the hall and climb up among them on the platform and thank them. You know, I shall never forget that, for it meant more to me than any distinction – it showed that the musicians liked me and were glad I had come, and I cannot tell you how happy it made me...

For the next ten years Mendelssohn travelled all over Europe and composed some of his greatest works. He especially loved England, although he was tired and over-worked when he wrote this letter.

MENDELSSOHN TO HIS MOTHER

London,
21 June 1842

...if this letter sounds rather weary and stiff-jointed, it merely reflects my feelings. They really have been driving me a little too hard; for a moment I feared that I should be stifled, there was such a crowd and such a throng round the organ. And a few days after that, when I had to play to an audience of 3,000 people in Exeter Hall, and they cheered me with 'Hurrahs' and waved their handkerchiefs and stamped their feet until the whole place rang with it – I noticed no ill effect at the time, but next morning my head felt dizzy, as though I had not slept. And then there is the sweet, pretty Queen Victoria, who is so girlish and shyly friendly and polite, and speaks German so well, and knows all my things so well – the four books of Songs Without Words, and those with words, and the Symphony, and the Song of Praise. Only yesterday evening I was at the Palace, where the Queen and Prince Albert were almost by themselves, and she sat down beside the piano while I played to her: first of all, seven Songs Without Words, then the Serenade, then two improvisations on *Rule Britannia* and on *Lützow's wilde Jagd* and *Gaudeamus igitur*. The last was a bit difficult to do, but I could hardly protest, and since she gave me the themes it was up to me to play them. All this and then the magnificent gallery in Buckingham Palace, where she drank tea and where there is a picture of two pigs by Paul Potter, and several others I found quite pleasant. And then the fact that they had very much liked my A Minor Symphony, that they had all welcomed us with a pleasant friendliness that surpassed anything I ever experienced in the way of hospitality

– all this sometimes makes my head positively spin, and I have to take myself firmly in hand so as not to lose my composure. ...

MENDELSSOHN TO FERDINAND SCHUBERT (BROTHER OF THE COMPOSER)

March 1845

Dear Professor:

Yesterday I received through Doctor Haertel the symphony sketch by your brother, of which you have made me the possessor. What pleasure you give me through so fine, so precious a gift, how deeply grateful I am to you for this remembrance of the deceased master, how honoured I feel that you present me so significant a specimen of his posthumous remains directly to me – all this you can surely put into words for yourself better than I, but I feel it necessary, although in few words, to express my gratitude to you for your gift. Believe me that I know how to esteem the magnificent gift at its true value, that you could have given it to no one who would have greater joy in it, who would be more sincerely grateful to you for it. In truth, it seems to me as if, through the very incompleteness of the work, the scattered half-finished indications, that I became at once personally acquainted with your brother more clearly and more intimately than I should have done through a completed piece. It seems as if I saw him there working in his room, and this joy I owe to your unexpectedly great kindness and generosity. Let me hope for an opportunity to meet you in the flesh, be it in Vienna or in this place here, and to make your personal acquaintance and then repeat to you by word of mouth, once again, all my thanks.

With respects
Yours faithfully,
Felix Mendelssohn-Bartholdy.
Frankfurt-am-Main,
22 March 1845

The symphony was the E minor, *Unfinished Symphony*. On his death Mendelssohn left the manuscript to his brother, Paul, who was to leave it on a train. However, it was retrieved and is now in the British Museum.

The first performance of *Elijah*, in 1846, under Mendelssohn's direction in Birmingham, is described to Paul. One year later, at the age of 38, Mendelssohn was to die of a heart attack in Leipzig..

MENDELSSOHN TO HIS BROTHER

Birmingham,
26 August 1846

...Never before has any of my pieces gone so splendidly at the first performance, or been so enthusiastically received by the musicians and the audience, as this Oratorio. It was clear during the first rehearsals in London, that they liked it and enjoyed singing and playing in it; but I confess that even I had not expected it to go with such a swing straight away when it was performed. If only you had been there! For the whole three and a half hours that it lasted, the big hall, with its 2,000 people, and the big orchestra, were so tensely concentrated on the one point at issue that not the faintest sound came from the audience, and I could sway that tremendous mass of orchestra and chorus and organ just as I wished. I thought of you so often! Especially when the rain-clouds gathered during the final chorus when everyone played and sang like mad, and after the first part was over and the whole passage was encored. No less than four choruses and four arias had to be repeated, and not one mistake was made in the whole of the first part – there were a few later, in the second part, but even those were trifling. A young English tenor sang the last aria so beautifully that I had to hold myself in so as to control my feelings and keep beating time properly. As I say, if only you had been there...

ROBERT SCHUMANN
1810-1856

Schumann was born in Zwickau in Saxony. His father was devoted to English Romantic writers, especially Scott and Byron, and was a bookseller and publisher.

Like Berlioz, Schumann went against his parents' wishes when he became a musician. They had pinned their hopes on him becoming a lawyer. It wasn't easy for him. He was a sensitive, introspective man. His struggle to gain the hand of his beloved Clara caused him considerable pain and ended in the law courts.

SCHUMANN TO HIS MOTHER

Heidelberg,
30 July 1830

...My *whole life* has been a *twenty-year-long battle* between poetry and prose, or if you prefer, between music and law. In practical matters my ideals were just as high as in art. My ideal was, in fact, to have a practical influence, and my hope, that I should have to wrestle with a wide sphere of action. But what prospect can there be of that, particularly in love of the cadging and money-grubbing that goes with a legal career! At Leipzig I was quite unconcerned about future plans; I went on my way, dreaming and loitering and really doing nothing worthwhile; since I came here I have done more work, but in both places my attachment to art has been growing deeper and deeper. Now I have come to the crossroads, and think with terror, 'Whither now?' If I follow my own instinct it will lead one to art, and I believe that is the right path. But really – do not take this amiss, I say it lovingly and in a whisper – I always felt as though you were barring my way in that direction, for worthy, motherly reasons that I could see as clearly as yourself – the 'uncertain future and unreliable living', as we used to put it. But what is to happen next? A man can have no more tormenting thought than the prospect of an unhappy, lifeless and superficial future for which he would have only himself to blame. But it is not easy, either, to choose a way of life in complete contrast to one's early upbringing and disposition; it requires patience, confidence and rapid training. I am as yet in the youth of my imagination, able to be cultivated and ennobled by art; and I have become convinced that with diligence and patience and a good teacher I shall be a match for any pianist, for the whole business of piano-playing is simply a matter of technique and nimbleness; now and then I have imagination too, and perhaps some creative ability...

Clara Wieck was the daughter of his friend and piano teacher. She was born in 1819 and was an accomplished concert pianist. Robert and Clara fell very much in love but Clara's father was totally against the marriage. Clara died in 1896.

SCHUMANN TO CLARA WIECK

18 September 1837

The interview with your father was terrible. Such coldness, such malice, such distraction, such contradictions – he has a new way of destroying one, he thrusts the knife into your heart up to the hilt...So what now, dearest Clara? I cannot tell what to do next. *I have no idea.* It baffles my understanding, and it is completely useless to approach your father on a matter of sentiment. So what now? So what now? Above all, arm yourself and *do not let yourself be sold*...I trust you, oh *with my whole heart*, indeed that is what sustains me – but you will have to be *very strong*, more than you have any idea. For your father gave me with his own lips the dreadful assurance that 'nothing would shake him'. You must fear everything from him; *he will overcome you by force* if he cannot do so by guile. So fear everything!

Today I feel so dead, so humiliated, that I can scarcely grasp one beautiful, pleasant thought; even your picture eludes me, so that I can scarcely remember your eyes. I have not grown faint-hearted, capable of giving you up; but so embittered, so offended in my most sacred feelings, reduced to the level of all that is most commonplace. If I only had a word from you. You must tell me what to do. Otherwise everything within me will turn to dust and ashes and I shall go away. To be forbidden to see you!...I try in vain to find some excuse for your father, as I have always thought him an honourable, kindly man. I try in vain to discern in his refusal some finer, deeper reason – such as that he may be afraid your art would suffer if you were prematurely betrothed, that you are altogether too young, and so forth. Nothing of the kind – believe me, he will throw you to the first comer who has enough money and position. His highest ambition is giving concerts and travelling; for that he oppresses you and shatters my strength just when I am trying to bring something beautiful into the world; for he laughs at all your tears…

But keep your eyes firmly on the goal. It is through your sweetness that you must achieve everything now, not through your strength. There is little or nothing I can do but keep silent, any new plea to your father would merely bring me fresh mortification. Brace yourself to decide what must be done. I will follow you like a child…But my head is in such a whirl; I feel like laughing out of desperation. This situation cannot last long, my nature could not endure it…My life has been torn up by the roots.

Afternoon of the same day
…I can see that everything now depends on our proceeding calmly and prudently. In the end he is bound to realise that he must give you up. His obstinacy will shatter against our love; *it must be so*, my Clara…

Hector Berlioz, whose *Symphonie Fantastique* had been praised by Robert Schumann in 1835, was introduced to Clara Wieck whilst she was in Paris. She was on a tour of Europe with a travelling companion, earning money by giving concerts and steeping herself in musical life. She described her meeting with Berlioz in a letter to Robert.

CLARA WIECK TO ROBERT SCHUMANN

Paris,
Spring 1839

He is quiet, has uncommonly thick hair, and is always looking at the floor, casting his eyes downward. He will visit me tomorrow. At first I didn't know it was he and wondered who this man was who continually spoke about you; finally I asked him his name, and when he told me I reacted with such happy astonishment that he must have been flattered. His new opera (*Benvenuto Cellini*) has been a complete failure.

Berlioz was too busy to do much to help her career whilst in Paris. His review of her concert on April 16 was luke-warm and Clara described it as 'extremely malicious.' Nevertheless, Clara was a success in Paris. However, she was under a great strain with her father who so strongly opposed the marriage between her and Robert. She had already decided to marry Robert with or without her father's permission at Easter 1840 but her father's influence was strong and she missed his support at this time of the tour.

SCHUMANN TO H. DORN

Leipzig,
September 1839

...It is indeed probable that my music bears many traces of the battles I have had to fight for Clara, and equally certain that you too will have understood it. She was almost the sole inspiration of the Concerto, the Sonatas, the *Davidbundler Dances*, the *Kreisleriana* and the *Novellettes*. But I have seldom come across anything more clumsy and shortsighted than what Rellstab wrote about my *Scenes of Childhood*. He supposes I took some screaming child as my model and then tried to find the right notes. It was the other way round. Though I do not deny that I saw a few children's faces in my mind's eye while I was composing; but the titles were added later, of course, and are really no more than slight pointers to the way of interpreting and playing the pieces...

The previous year Schumann had visited Vienna where he found the manuscript of Schubert's *Symphony in C major* (*The Great*) in the house of Schubert's brother, Ferdinand. It was sent to Mendelssohn, who conducted the first performance in the Leipzig *Gewandhaus*. Here Schumann describes the rehearsal to Clara.

SCHUMANN TO CLARA WIECK

Leipzig,
11 December 1839

...Clara, today I have been in the seventh heaven. At the rehearsal they played a symphony by Franz Schubert. If only you had been there! For I cannot describe it to you; all the instruments were like human voices, and immensely full of life and wit, and the instrumentation, regardless of Beethoven and the length, the divine length, like a four-volume novel, longer than the Ninth Symphony. I was utterly happy, with nothing left to wish for except that you were my wife and that I could write such symphonies myself...

RICHARD WAGNER
1813 – 1883

Wilhelm Richard Wagner was born in Leipzig and died in Venice aged nearly seventy, after a turbulent life, personally, politically and musically. He was brought up in a theatrical family and became deeply interested in theatre and drama. Part of his schooldays were spent at St Thomas's School, Leipzig, where eighty years earlier Bach had taught.

His music drama was an expression of the German Romantic Movement and his influence on composition, opera and the presentation of opera was enormous, breaking new ground. In 1872 he designed and supervised the building of the Festival Theatre at Bayreuth, still a miracle today.

He said, 'The musicians must not lose a single inch. An orchestra must not feel cramped, if it is to take pleasure in playing well. This is more important than anything else.'

He achieved this with an acoustically perfect wooden auditorium in which the audience was able to concentrate entirely on the action on the stage, with the orchestra out of sight and the auditorium in darkness.

In the following proposal to the music publisher, Schott, the 17 year old Wagner illustrates his self-confidence and tenacity.

WAGNER TO SCHOTT

6, October 1830

Sir,

Beethoven's last magnificent symphony has long been the object of my deepest study. The more I came to realise its greatness, the more it saddened me that it should remain so misunderstood, so neglected by the majority of the musical public. A suitable piano arrangement seemed to me the best way to make this masterpiece more accessible. To my great regret I have so far not found one (for the inadequacy of Czerny's arrangement for four hands is obvious). My own enthusiasm then prompted me to undertake an arrangement of this symphony *for two hands*, and so far I have managed to set the first and perhaps most difficult movement, with the greatest possible clarity and attention to detail. I therefore approach your respected publishing house now, to enquire whether you would be interested in such an arrangement (for you will appreciate that without your encouragement I should not feel inclined to persevere with this laborious task). As soon as I hear of your interest, I shall proceed and complete what I have begun without delay. I therefore ask you most respectfully for an early reply, humbly assuring you of my most earnest diligence.

I am, Sir, Your obedient servant, Richard Wagner

Schott did not reply and when Wagner sent a reminder, they turned the proposal down. Unperturbed, Wagner completed the arrangement and in 1832 sent it back to the publisher asking for no fee but for a gift of four Beethoven scores instead. Schotts did not publish the work, but did send Wagner the music he wanted.

From Paris Wagner moved to Dresden and shortly became conductor of the Opera. Here he wrote *Tannhäuser* and *Lohengrin*. In 1849 he had to flee Dresden for Zurich as a result of his participation in the failed rebellion of 1848. During Wagner's exile in Switzerland, Liszt remained a loyal friend and admirer.

Some insight into Wagner's passion and creative energy, and his shortage of money, are shown in a letter to his friend Ferdinand Heine in Dresden.

WAGNER TO FERDINAND HEINE

Zürich,
19 November 1849

...In short, I have been living for more than three months on a few hundred florins advanced to me by a local friend, and which represents the utmost he could manage. After the end of this month I simply do not know how I am to live at all...

...If I can avoid outside disturbances I shall create work after work – for I am overflowing with material and artistic projects...

...My *Lohengrin* was completed long ago and I am longing heart and soul to write at last the music for my *Siegfried*.

...So that the only thing that matters to me is to *gain time*, i.e. to *gain life*. Unfortunately for me I have no trade by which to earn my daily bread: as things are, it *must* be given to me, so that I can remain an artist. Who will do this? Only those who love me – who love me, my work and my artistic aims and efforts so much that they set store by preserving my art and enabling me to continue my artistic efforts...

In 1850 Liszt produced the first performance of *Lohengrin* in Weimar. This was the start of Wagner's fame and began the ever-growing demand for his works in the opera houses of Germany. Unfortunately it was not safe for Wagner to return to Germany for the performance.

LISZT TO WAGNER

Weimar,
July 1850

Your *Lohengrin* will be performed in the most exceptional conditions, with every possible prospect of success. The management is spending nearly 2,000 thalers on the production, a thing that has never before happened at Weimar in living memory. The Press is not being forgotten, and serious, well-informed articles are to appear one after another in various newspapers. Everyone in the theatre will be aflame with enthusiasm.

I shall take charge of all rehearsals, piano, chorus and orchestra; Genast will follow your instructions for the staging with warmth and vigour. It goes without saying that we shall not cut a single note, a single iota, from your work, and that to the best of our ability we shall present it in all its beauty.

I now come to a matter that distresses me, but which I feel it my duty not to conceal from you. It is quite impossible for you to return to Germany or to come to Weimar for the performance of *Lohengrin*. Next time we meet I shall be able to give you the details; to do so in writing would take too long and serve no useful purpose...

Wagner began work on his immense *Tetralogy*, the four-evening music drama *The Ring of the Nibelung* (*Rhinegold*, *The Valkyrie*, *Siegfried* and *The Twilight of the Gods*).

WAGNER TO THEODOR UHLIG

Albisbrunn,
12 November 1851

...With this new concept I sever all connection with our present-day theatre and its audience: I make a definite and permanent break with present-day forms. Would you like to know what my intentions are regarding my plan? In the first place, *to carry it out*, so far as lies in my power as poet and composer. This will take me at least three full years.

I cannot look for a performance until *after the revolution*; only revolution can bring the artists and audiences to me; the next revolution must necessarily put an end to our whole system of theatre management; it must and will collapse, that is inevitable. And out of its ruins I can call forth what I require; *then* I shall find out what I need. I shall then build a theatre on the Rhine and send out invitations to a great dramatic festival; after a year's preparation I shall give a performance of my entire work, spread over four days. In this way I shall reveal to the men of the revolution the significance of their revolution in its noblest sense. *That audience* will understand me, as the present-day public is incapable of doing.

However extravagant this plan may be, it is the one to which I am now devoting my whole life, my writing and my endeavours. If I live to see it carried out, I shall have had a splendid life: if not, I shall have died for something beautiful. But only this can give me any pleasure now!

> Wagner was optimistic *The Tetralogy* was not finished for twenty-two years; and it was twenty-five years before his new theatre, the famous Wagner Festival Theatre, was opened in Bayreuth.
>
> His banishment from Germany ended in 1859. He was deeply in debt when he was rescued by the young King Ludwig of Bavaria who enabled him to settle in Bayreuth and complete his dream of building his theatre.
>
> Wagner's first marriage to Minna was tempestuous and ended in divorce in 1861. Wagner and Cosima Bülow, the daughter of Franz Liszt and wife of Hans von Bülow, had a passionate affair and had three children: Isolde born in 1865, Eva born in 1867 and Siegfried (Fidi) born in 1869. In 1868 Cosima left her husband to live with Wagner and her children, and in 1870 she was divorced and actually married Wagner.

WAGNER TO COSIMA

Bayreuth,
24 April 1872

What bliss when I can show everything here to the children!...How they will love the opera house! O, if only you were here, but let the mama not overtax herself!...O, now kiss our children and love, love, love me! I breathe with you and foresee great blessings in you!...O my love, my love! How lovely you are!...Blessings on our Fidi! Blessings on all the loved ones so full of life! But – their mother! O that mother! I sense her blessing and I am blissfully happy!

Amongst the visitors to the opening of the Festival Theatre in Bayreuth in 1876 was the French novelist Judith Gautier. When she left Bayreuth after the first festival, Wagner arranged to correspond clandestinely.

Bayreuth,
September 1876

By the way, you can write to me directly; I have taken care of everything. Herr Schappauf [Wagner's barber] will be our intermediary. I would love to have just a line from you, especially since you are always before my eyes, here to my right on the sofa (my God, those eyes!), while I was writing souvenir notes for my poor lady singers. O how incredible it all is: you are the cornucopia, the overfulfilment of my life which has been so peaceful and protected since Cosima came to me. You are my largesse, my intoxicating superfluity! (Neatly put, don't you think?) But what does it matter – you understand me. Adieu, Judith!

GIUSEPPE VERDI
1813-1901

Verdi was the son of a village innkeeper and was born near Busseto in the district of Parma. He was refused entry to the Conservatory in Milan, 'lacking aptitude for music.' He stayed in Milan, studying privately, supported by a grant from a charitable institution. After he had completed his studies he returned to his home where he worked as a general music practitioner. At twenty four he went back to Milan with an opera that he had written. It was performed at La Scala. It is now forgotten but other operas followed in a steady stream, including *Rigoletto*, *Il Trovatore* and *La Traviata*. *Aida* was to follow in 1871, *Othello* in 1877 when he was aged seventy three.

Verdi was commissioned to write an opera for Naples but had difficulty in selecting a suitable subject. However, in 1857 he began working with Antonio Somma as librettist, on *Gustave III of Sweden*. Eventually, because of repeated problems with the censors, this was to become an opera about a Governor of colonial Boston (*Un Ballo in Maschera*). Some of Verdi's letters during this transformation vividly express his frustration.

VERDI TO ANTONIO SOMMA

17 November, 1857

...Yesterday, your letter of the 14th reached me, with the memorandum from the Neapolitan censor enclosed. They will allow the action to be placed, it says, anywhere in the north except for Sweden or Norway. But in what century must the action take place? Give me some ideas about this. To find a period that will justify a readiness to believe in witches, as requested by His Excellency the Censor, will not be easy...

> Somma suggested that the opera be set in the twelfth-century in Pomerania, but Verdi thought the period too remote.

...I really think the twelfth century is a little too remote for our Gustave. It is such a raw and brutal period, especially in those countries, that it seems a serious contradiction to use it as a setting for characters conceived in the French style as Gustave and Oscar are, and for such a splendid drama based on customs near our own time. We shall have to find some great prince or duke, a rogue whether of the North or not, who has seen something of the world and caught something of the atmosphere of the court of Louis XIV...

> The opera, now called *La vendetta in domino* was finished in December and delivered in January 1858. The setting was now seventeenth-century Pomerania, but the censors were not happy with the thinly disguised names, country and time of Gustave III and his assassination.

VERDI TO ANTONIO SOMMA

Naples,
7 February 1858

...I am drowning in a sea of troubles. It's almost certain the censors will forbid our libretto. I don't know why. I was quite right to warn you to avoid every sentence, every word which could offend. They began by objecting to certain phrases and words, and then entire scenes and finally the whole subject. They made the following suggestions but only as a special favour:

(1) Change the hero into an ordinary gentleman, with no suggestion of sovereignty.
(2) Change the wife into a sister.
(3) Alter the scene with the fortune-teller, and put it back to a time when people believed in such things.

(4) No ball.

(5) The murder to be off-stage.

(6) Omit the scene of the drawing of the name.

And so on, and so on, and so on!!

As you can imagine, these changes are out of the question, so no more opera. So the subscribers won't pay the last two instalments, so the government will withdraw the subsidy, so the directors will sue everyone, and already threaten me with damages of 50,000 ducats. What hell!! Write and give me your opinion of all this.

Somma replied.

...Make whatever use of my poetry seems best to you. Delete and revise as the censor requires, if there is time, retaining what they permit, and rewriting scenes and dialogue when the censor demands it. Do whatever is necessary to please these gentlemen: *but I insist on two things*: one, that instead of my name on the title page there should appear that of someone else; merely to remain anonymous is no longer sufficient for me, after it has been announced to everyone that I am the author of the libretto; two, that the opera be no longer entitled *La vendetta in domino*, but something else, whatever you like.

> The dispute continued; Verdi refused to accept a libretto altered by the opera house management to satisfy the censors. After a law suit, Verdi was released from his contract and allowed to keep the opera to use elsewhere. Verdi decided to try and present it in Rome, but the censors still objected to details of the plot and insisted it be set outside Europe. Somma at last agreed to Verdi's suggestion: 'What would you think of North America at the time of the English domination?' *Un Ballo in Maschera*, set in Boston, Massachusetts at the end of the seventeenth century, in which only an English governor, not a King, was assassinated, received its first performance in Rome in 1859.
>
> No matter how great was Verdi's reputation, it did not prevent one ordinary opera goer from criticising the master and even, in a letter of supreme presumption, asking for his money back. In his reply Verdi showed his generous sense of humour.

PROSPERO BERTANI TO VERDI

Reggio (Emelia),
7 May 1872

Much honoured Signor Verdi,

On the 2nd of this month I went to Parma, drawn there by the sensation made by your opera *Aida*. So great was my curiosity that half an hour before the commencement of the performance I was already in my seat, no. 120. I admired the scenery, I heard with pleasure the excellent singers, and I did all in my powers to let nothing escape me. At the end of the opera, I asked myself if I was satisfied, and the answer was 'No'. I started back to Reggio, and listened in the railway carriage to the opinions of my fellow travellers, nearly all of whom agreed in considering *Aida* a work of the first order.

I was therefore seized with the idea of hearing it again, and on the 4th I returned to Parma. I made unprecedented efforts to get a reserved seat. As the crowd was enormous I was obliged to spend five lire to witness the performance in any comfort.

I came to this conclusion about it: it is an opera in which there is absolutely nothing thrilling or exciting. Without the pomp of the spectacle, the public would not sit through to the end. When it has filled the theatre a few more times, it will be banished to the dust of the archives.

You can picture to yourself, my dear Signor Verdi, my regret at having spent on two occasions thirty-two lire. Add to this the aggravating circumstance that I am dependent on my family, and that this money preys on my mind like a frightened spectre. I therefore address myself frankly to you in order that you may send me the amount. The account is as follows:

Railroad – one way	2.60 lire
Railroad – return	3.30
Theatre	8.00
Detestable supper at station	2.00
	15.00
Twice	X2
	31.90

Hoping you will deliver me from this embarrassment, I salute you from my heart.

Prospero Bertani

Letter from Monteverdi to the Marchese
Enzo Bentivoglio dated September, 1627.
In it he discusses the problems of setting to
music a libretto forming part of a wedding
celebration at Parma.

Portrait of Monteverdi by Bernardo Strozzi

Testimonial for Therese Kaufmann,
March 17, 1823.

Beethoven, from the oil portrait by
W. J. Mähler, 1815.

Letter from Monteverdi to the Marchese
Enzo Bentivoglio dated September, 1627.
In it he discusses the problems of setting to
music a libretto forming part of a wedding
celebration at Parma.

Portrait of Monteverdi by Bernardo Strozzi

Testimonial for Therese Kaufmann,
March 17, 1823.

Beethoven, from the oil portrait by
W. J. Mähler, 1815.

A letter by Schumann to a young woman, 1843.

Robert Schumann

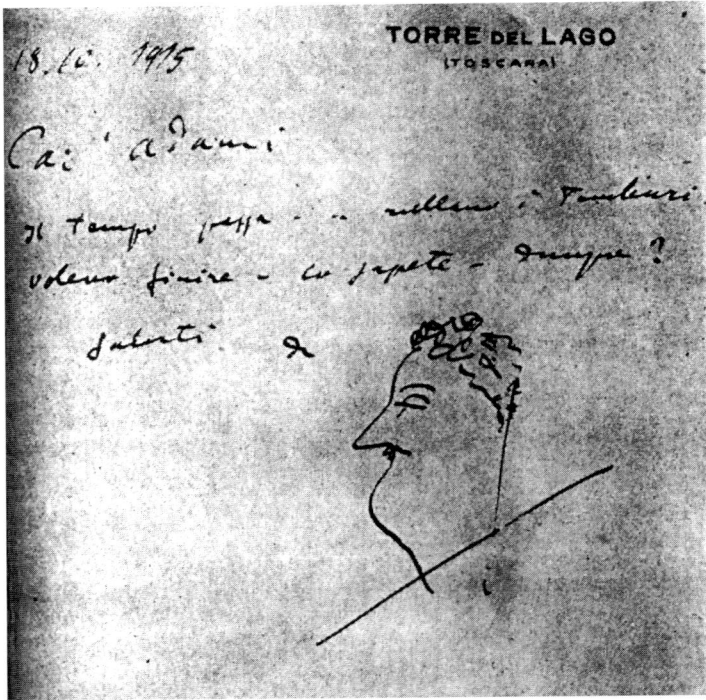

A curious letter, signed by Puccini with a
caricature sketch of his own head.

Giacomo Puccini.

y trouvera peut-être quelques rares sympathies ; les cœurs déchirés s'y reconnaîtront. Un tel morceau est incompréhensible pour la plupart des Français, et absurde et insensé pour des Italiens.

En sortant de la représentation d'Hamlet, épouvanté de ce que j'y avais ressenti, je m'étais promis formellement de ne pas m'exposer de nouveau à la flamme Shakespearienne. Le lendemain on afficha Romeo and Juliet .... J'avais mes entrées à l'orchestre de l'Odéon ; eh bien, dans la crainte que de nouveaux ordres donnés au concierge du théâtre ne vinssent m'empêcher de m'y introduire comme à l'ordinaire, aussitôt après avoir vu l'annonce du redoutable Drame, je courus au bureau de location acheter une stalle pour m'assurer ainsi doublement de mon entrée. Il n'en fallait pas tant pour m'achever.

Après la mélancolie, les navrantes douleurs, l'amour éploré, les ironies cruelles, les noires méditations, les brisements de cœur, la folie, les larmes, les deuils, les catastrophes, les sinistres hasards d'Hamlet, après les sombres nuages, les vents glacés du Danemarck, m'exposer à l'ardent soleil, aux nuits ~~enivrantes et~~ embaumées de l'Italie, assister au spectacle de cet amour prompt comme la pensée ; brûlant comme la lave, impérieux, irrésistible, immense, et pur et beau comme le sourire des anges, à ces scènes furieuses de vengeances, à ces étreintes éperdues, à ces luttes désespérées de l'amour et de la mort, c'était trop. aussi, dès le troisième acte, tombant brisé à genoux sur un siège placé devant moi, respirant à peine, et souffrant comme si une main de fer m'eût ~~étreint~~ le cœur, je me dis avec une entière conviction : ah ! je suis perdu. Il faut ajouter que je ne savais pas alors un seul mot d'anglais, que je n'entrevoyais Shakespeare qu'au travers des brouillards de la traduction de Letourneur et que je n'apercevais

A page of Berlioz's memoirs written in his own hand.

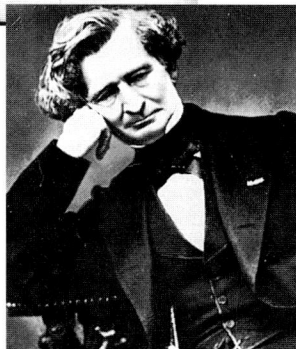

Berlioz, by Petit, 1863.

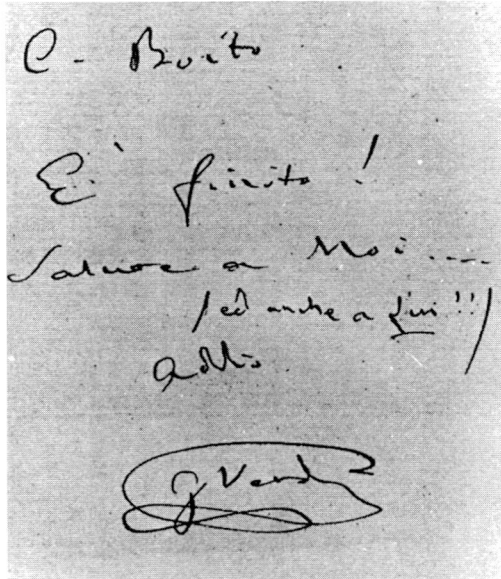

Verdi writing to the poet and musician
Boito, who arranged the libretto for *Otello*.
It reads:
'Dear Boito, it's finished!
Greetings to us…
(and also to Him!!)
Farewell!'

Giuseppe Verdi

Letter to Ernest Chausson.

Debussy at 18, during his stay at Florence with Madame von Meck.

Letter from Tchaikovsky to Madame von Meck, written from San Remo in January, 1878. He has nearly finished *Eugene Onegin* and was writing loving, intense letters.

Tchaikovsky with his nephew Vladimir (Bob) Davidov, to whom he dedicated the *Pathétique* Symphony.

Verdi forwarded it to his publisher, Ricordi, with a covering note:

You may well imagine that to protect the son of a family from the frightful spectres which pursue him, I shall willingly pay the little bill which he sends me. I therefore beg you to forward by one of your representatives the sum of 27.80 lire to this Signor Prosper Berating, Via San Dominica, No. 5, Reggio. It isn't the entire sum that he demands, but – to pay for his supper too! – certainly not! He could very well have eaten at home!!!!! It is understood that he must send you a receipt, and a note in which he must undertake to attend no new opera of mine, thus avoiding for himself that threat of spectres, and sparing me further travelling expenses.

> Verdi was seldom content with his work and frequently re-wrote his operas. In the following letter he discusses *Simon Boccanegra* with his publisher, Giulio Ricordi.

20 November 1880

The score as it stands is impossible. Too gloomy, too depressing! There is no need to touch anything in the first Act or in the last...But Act II will have to be entirely rewritten, to give it more vigour and variety, put more life into it. Musically speaking, one might keep the *cavatina* of the soprano, the duet with the tenor and the other duet between the father and daughter, although they are *cabalettas*!! (Let the earth swallow me!) *Cabalettas* * don't shock me so much as all that, and if a young man should come along tomorrow who could write one as good – for instance – as *Meco tu vieni o misera* or *Ah perchè non posso odiarti,* I should listen to it with all my heart and be glad to forget all the sophistical quibbles and affectations of our clever orchestrations. Ah, progress, learning, realism...! Ah, ah! Be as realistic as you like, but...Shakespeare was a realist, but he didn't know it. His realism was inspired; ours is planned, calculated. So what difference does it make; if we must have a system I prefer the *cabalettas*. The worst of it is that in its rage for progress, art is going backwards. Art without spontaneity, naturalness and simplicity is no longer art...

*elaborate ending of an aria

JOHANNES BRAHMS
1833–1897

Brahms was the son of a double-bass player and was born in Hamburg. As a young man he played in cafes and dancing-halls. Whilst touring with a Jewish Hungarian violinist, he came to the notice of Liszt and later Schumann. The friendship that developed between Schumann and his wife Clara and Brahms was very important to him and after Schumann's attempted suicide he moved into their house in Dusseldorf and helped to care for the family with their seven children.

Dvorak was another composer whom Brahms was to befriend. Brahms was a warm admirer of his music and became a generous and altruistic friend. They were very different. On the one hand we have Brahms the North German Protestant, bachelor and city-dweller, with a strong interest in philosophical matters and on the other hand Dvorak, a Roman Catholic, devout family man with little formal learning in the fields of literature and philosophy. When Dvorak applied for a State grant for 'young, poor and talented painters, sculptors and musicians' in 1877, Brahms supported his application and the following correspondence was started which included Brahms' letters to Simrock, his own publisher in Berlin (one of the leading publishers of the day). The first letter is from Dvorak to Brahms:

3 December 1877

...At the suggestion of the esteemed Prof. Hanslick I venture to address these few lines to you, honoured Master, in order to express to you my deep-felt thanks for the kindness you have shown me.

What I count a still greater happiness, however, is the sympathy you have been good enough to accord to my modest talent and the favour with which (as Prof. Hanslick tells me) you received my Czech vocal duets [the Moravian Duets]. Prof. Hanslick now advises me to procure a German translation of these songs which you, dear Sir, would be so kind as to recommend to your publishers. It is my duty to address myself to you with one more request – that you should be good enough to be of assistance to me in this matter which, for me, is of such great importance. It would be, indeed, not only for me but also for my beloved country, of immeasurable value if you, honoured master, whose works delight in such great measure the whole musical world, would give me such an introduction.

With the earnest request that I may continue in the future to enjoy your highly valued favour, I beg your kind permission to forward to you for your inspection some of my chamber music works and compositions for orchestra....

Brahms replied shortly afterwards in the same month:

[undated]

...Allow me quite shortly to thank you for your lines and for the great pleasure I have derived from the works you sent me. I have taken the liberty of writing about them, and especially about the 'Duets', to Mr Fritz Simrock...

From the title it would appear that the Duets are still your property, in German translation. Can you manage that? In any case I beg you not to rush the matter so that the work may not suffer in consequence. In the meantime you could perhaps send the folio to Mr. Simrock to have a look at? The rest will follow ...

Brahms was as good as his word and the following is his recommendation to Simrock.

12 December 1877

Dear Simrock,

In connection with the State Grant, I have for several years now been rejoicing over the works of Anton Dvorak (pr. Dworshak) of Prague. This year he sends me amongst others a book of ten duets for two sopranos with pianoforte, which seems to me very pretty and practical for publication. He appears to have had this book printed at his own expense. The title and unfortunately also the words are Bohemian only. I induced him to send the songs to you. When you play them through you will be as pleased as I am, and as a publisher, be especially pleased with the piquancy of them. Very likely many of the words have already been translated by (the lately deceased) Wenzig. Otherwise, perhaps Dr. Siegfried Kapper of Prague would be the best one to do them. Dvorak has written every possible thing, operas (Bohemian), symphonies, quartets and pianoforte pieces. Anyway he is a very talented man. Almost poor! And I ask you to consider this! That the duets are good will be evident to you, and they would be 'a good article'. The address is Prague, Kornthorsgase No. 10, ii.

Best wishes,

Yours,

J. Br.

Dvorak sent the Duets to Simrock and thus begun a successful business connection between the two men which later developed into a friendship. Sometime in December 1877 Dvorak travelled to Vienna in order to meet Brahms and thank him personally for the introduction. Sadly, Brahms was away on a concert tour, so in the New Year Dvorak wrote to him.

23 January 1878

...And now I venture, highly honoured Master, to approach you with a request. Permit me, out of gratitude and a deep respect for your incomparable musical works, to offer you the dedication of my D minor Quartet.

It would be for me the highest honour I can aspire to and I should be the happiest of men to have the honour to subscribe myself as bound to you in eternal gratitude...

Brahms to Dvorak, in reply:

March 1978

I regret extremely that I was away from home when you were here. The more so as I have such an aversion to letter-writing that I cannot hope to make up for it in the least by correspondence. And, today, no more than to say that to occupy myself with your things gives me the greatest pleasure, but that I would give a good deal to be able to discuss individual points with you personally. You write somewhat hurriedly. When you are filling in the numerous missing sharps, flats and naturals, then it would be good to look a little more closely at the notes themselves and at the voice parts, etc.

Forgive me, but it is very desirable to point out such things to a man like you. I also accept the works just as they are very gratefully and consider myself honoured by the dedication of the quartet.

I think it would be very good if you gave me both the quartets that I know. If Simrock should not be willing, might I try to place them elsewhere?

And again Brahms prods Simrock regarding Dvorak:

...I don't know what further risk you are wanting to take with this man. I have no idea about business or what interest there is for larger works. I do not care to make recommendations, because I have only my eyes and my ears and they are altogether my own. If you should think of going on with it at all, get him to send you his two string quartets, major and minor, and have them played to you. The best that a musician can have Dvorak has, and it is in these compositions....

In the following letter Brahms (who has admitted to Dvorak that he dislikes writing letters) expresses a sneaking feeling that many of us have when reading other people's private letters. He is responding to a request from Maria Lipsius, the editor of *Musikerbriefe* for permission to publish some of his letters in a collection.

BRAHMS TO MARIA LIPSIUS

Vienna,
27 May 1885

Dear Madam,

To be sure, I have the courage to ask you not to print the letters in question. I know and admit that I invariably write reluctantly, hurriedly and carelessly; but when I see an example like yours, I feel ashamed.

It takes a kind of courage to write to an unknown, cultivated and sympathetic man in such a slipshod style as I did in this instance.

But to allow such letters to be printed, to give one's explicit agreement, would be something other than courage!

If you will allow me to say categorically, here and now, that no-one could give me greater displeasure than by printing any letter of mine – I will gladly make an exception of this particular one.

You can include it in your book all the more readily, because it will show your readers that it is not you but I who bear the blame for the absence of others, and because I am careful not to draw any conclusion from your proposal to include my own letters, regarding the other contents and the value of your book.

I know, not merely from 'Schiller and Goethe' but from the most agreeable personal experience as well, that there are plenty of people who enjoy letter-writing and write good ones.

But there are others like myself, and their letters–if the writer deserves it in other respects – should be read and interpreted indulgently and warily.

For instance, I am delighted to have a letter of Beethoven's to treasure as a relic; but it makes me shudder to think how much such a letter is supposed to signify and explain!

The same applies to unpublished works a musician leaves behind him. I have always followed up such things eagerly, studied them, copied and re-copied them. For instance, I have cherished the uncounted surplus evidences of their industry and genius left by Haydn and by Franz Schubert.

I have always wished that such valuable and instructive treasures might be copied for the large libraries, where they would be accessible to people seriously interested in them. I will not dwell on the very different feelings with which I see those beloved treasures in print – or arrange them for publication myself, to make sure it will at least be done as decently as possible!

The amount of misunderstanding and misinterpretation that occurs in such cases is quite unbelievable, and whether such publications are necessary, desirable or superfluous and even harmful – I do not know!

At the risk that you will regard the beginning of this letter as sheer hypocrisy,

I sign myself,

Yours respectfully and devotedly,

J. Brahms

PETER ILYICH TCHAIKOVSKY
1840–1893

Tchaikovsky was born in the Urals, the son of a mining engineer. He came from an unmusical family, although he did take piano lessons as a child. When he was nineteen, Tchaikovsky became clerk Grade One in the Ministry of Justice. To relieve the monotony of his job he joined a choral class, which he enjoyed so much that he then decided to take piano lessons again and gradually became interested in composition. He then left his job and studied at the Conservatoire at St Petersburg.

A student from the Conservatoire, Antonina Milyukova, fell in love with Tchaikovsy and sent him the following declaration:

ANTONINA MILYUKOVA TO TCHAIKOVSKY

May 1877

I've been in the most agonising state for a whole week, Pyotr Ilich, not knowing whether to write to you or not. I see that my letters are already beginning to be wearisome to you. But will you really break off this correspondence with me, not having seen me even once? No, I am convinced you will not be so cruel. Do you, maybe, take me for a frivolous person or a gullible girl, and therefore place no trust in my letters? How can I prove to you that my words are genuine, and that ultimately I could not lie in such a matter? After your last letter I loved you twice as much again, and your shortcomings mean absolutely nothing to me.

Perhaps if you were a perfect being I would have remained completely cool towards you. I am dying of longing, and I burn with a desire to see you, to sit with you and talk with you, though I also fear that at first I shan't be in a state to utter a word. There is no failing that might cause me to fall out-of-love with you ....

Having today sent a man to deliver my letter to you, I was very surprised to learn that you had left Moscow, and longing descended upon me even more. I sit at home all day, pace the room from corner to corner like a crazy thing, thinking only of that moment when I shall see you. I shall be ready to throw myself on your neck, to smother you with kisses – but what right have I to do this? Maybe, indeed, you take this for effrontery on my part....

I can assure you that I am a respectable and honourable woman in the full sense of the word, and I have nothing that I would wish to conceal from you. My first kiss will be given to you and to no one else in the world. Farewell, my dear one. Do not try to disillusion me further about yourself, because you are only wasting your time. I cannot live without you, and so maybe soon I shall kill myself. So let me see you and kiss you so that I may remember that kiss in the other world. Farewell. Yours eternally, A.M....

The day before yesterday my letter was already written, and only today am I sending it, for I assume that you have still not returned to Moscow. Again I implore you: come to me. If you knew how I suffer then probably out of pity alone you would grant my request.

> Tchaikovsky had just started work on what was to be his greatest opera, *Eugene Onegin*, from Pushkin's novel, and he had begun by writing the music for the famous 'letter scene'. In fact, he composed like a man possessed – identifying totally with the character of Tatyana, the writer of the letter. He later admitted that he was in love with this character and despised Onegin's callous treatment of her. Therefore, when Tchaikovsy received a second letter from Antonina, some kind of emotional confusion set in. He met her for the first time on June 1. A day or two later he proposed and was accepted. The next month they were married. By September she had driven him to attempt a kind of indirect suicide by standing in the river as long as he could in the hope of catching pneumonia. They were separated shortly afterwards. She died in a lunatic asylum...
>
> He found independence through a stroke of luck – meeting the wealthy Madame Nadezhda von Meck, who admired his composition and offered to give him a yearly allowance. In the following letter to her we hear of his opinion of Berlioz. He then writes to Anatoli on the same subject.

TCHAIKOVSKY TO MME VON MECK

12-24 February 1879

I am not an absolute admirer of Berlioz. There is something incomplete in the organization of his music, a lack of knowledge of how to choose harmonies and modulations. There is an element of "wanting to please" in him which I cannot accept. But this does not prevent his having the spirit of a fine artist and sometimes he reaches the greatest heights. Some of the Scenes in *Faust* – especially that on the banks of the Elbe are real pearls of his. Yesterday when I listened I only stopped my sobs with difficulty. Mephistopheles' recitative is charming, and so too the chorus of sprites and the Dance of the Sylphides. As one listens to this music one feels that he was full of poetic inspiration...

Paris
12-24 February 1879

As I was writing the date on this letter I realized that it will be twenty years since I ended my studies at the College. What an old man I am, Tolia! But (spit, spit, spit) the old man's health is good...

Last night I had a most enjoyable artistic experience. I heard the whole of the *Damnation de Faust* which is one of the miracles of art. Several times I had to suppress my sobs. The devil only knows what a curious man Berlioz is. On the whole his musical nature does not attract me and I cannot agree with the ugliness of some of his harmonies and modulation, but sometimes he reaches extraordinary heights. If you do not know the music I mean, ask Larocke – it is one of his favourites.

As Alesha has been behaving very well I promised to take him to the circus, in spite of being tired; but I could not put it off as it was the last day of Shrovetide. We got seats with great difficulty, had to sit very high up, and breathe a tropical atmosphere. The dear clown, Billy Haiden (the one you liked so much), was very funny. But I could not endure the whole performance and went home long before the end. The greatest pleasure I have in Paris is to sit at home in the evenings and enjoy absolute quiet in my back-yard.

Nadezhda Filaretovna sent me a mass of books. Today I simply had to get a ticket to the Theatre Francais where they are showing my favourite comedy, *Le Gendre de M. Poirier*. We saw it with Modia in 1876 and enjoyed it immensely. Tell him that the actors are the same as we saw then. I am going to the Post Office to see if there is a letter from one of you. There ought to be one from Modest. Tolia! It will be heavenly to get out of here and meet both of you, my dear ones. I am staying here only two weeks more. Judging by the way work has been going I will be able to finish the opera in the rough. Have you read Nikolin's story *A Specialist* in the *News of Europe* ? If not, get it and read it. It is about a divorce case. Very interesting. I kiss you with all my might.

Yours
P. Tchaikovsky

TCHAIKOVSKY TO MODEST TCHAIKOVSKY

Prague,
10-22 February 1888

Golubchik, Modia!

To write was impossible. My stay in Prague is quite an epic. I think some mention of it will be made in the papers and you will soon read about it; if not, you'll have to wait till I return and tell you everything. I should never have thought anything like it possible. The second concert took place yesterday, and after it they put on the second act of *Swan Lake*, which was beautifully staged. My success was absolutely terrific. During my ten days' stay I made a multitude of speeches, and at a big banquet on the day of my concert a speech in Czech.

On the whole the Czechs are very nice and some of those who have been with me everywhere I have learned to love. Charming Ziloty was with me all the time, looking after me like a nanny, and several times he saved me from complete exhaustion. P. Yurgenson also came here and stayed for five days. I was very glad to see him. They both left an hour ago and I am leaving for Paris tonight. It is impossible to describe how tired I am; one can only wonder how I could have stood up to it all without ruining my health. Of course, there were also many delightful moments, and I could never dream of having such success in Russia.

I have made friends with Dvorak and all the other composers. I must also add that the Czechs are great chaps – the open way in which they showed their sympathy for Russia in connection with my visit was wonderful. Please write to Paris, 14 Rue Richepanse. I am sending you three of my portraits from the papers. As to the papers, it is impossible to send them all; for the last ten days they have been absolutely overflowing. I embrace you.

P. Tchaikovsky

Hamburg
25 February–12 March 1889

Dear Modia

I have not written for a long time, but you probably read my letter to Bobik. In spite of a poor orchestra the Geneva Concert was an immense success. The Theatre was filled to overflowing, I was presented with a gilded wreath from the Russian colony, and all was as it should be. I left the next day, and was a bit sorry to do so as the weather was lovely: real spring. I am here since yesterday evening, and the first rehearsal took place today.

Brahms stayed an extra day to hear my symphony [Symphony No. 5] and was very kind. We had lunch together after the rehearsal and quite a few drinks. He is very sympathetic and I like his honesty and open mindedness. Neither he nor the players liked the Finale, which I also think rather horrible.

I will not say anything about my boredom, sadness, and despondency; it is still the same. All the time I count the days and hours until I am free. My letter to Bob crossed with his, as I wrote to him on the same day he had written to me. This time his letter is charming, not at all a letter to an old uncle one should please.

I am very glad that you have started to write a play. What a pity about poor Mania!!! The concert in London will be not on the 8th as I thought but on the 11th.

Going from here straight to Paris. Hope not to feel so bored there. So, write to Rue Richpanse 14.

I kiss you and embrace Kolia.
P. Tchaikovsky

What a shame that the Russian papers do not mention my concerts at all.

He then writes again, not sure whether or not he has already written. He sounds sad and lonely and rather old, although, in fact, he was only forty-nine.

TCHAIKOVSKY TO MODEST TCHAIKOVSKY

Hanover
5–17 March 1889

I do not remember, Modia, if I wrote from Hamburg. Did I tell you that Brahms stayed an extra day to hear my symphony and sat through the whole of the rehearsal? Also that we had a good time with him afterwards and that he liked the symphony (but not all of it), etc. etc.? There were three more rehearsals after the first – the fourth with audience and tickets. The players by degrees came to appreciate the symphony more and more, and at the last rehearsal they gave me an ovation. The concert was also a success. Best of all – I have stopped disliking the symphony. I love it again. Two days before the concert I was at Laub's Benefit (the one who plays in Pavlovsk) and after the two opening movements of the *Serenade* the audience gave me an ovation and the players one all of their own.

All this is very nice and fills my thoughts for the time being, but as soon as there are no rehearsals and no concerts I start getting into the usual state of gloom and boredom. Yesterday when I woke up I was in utter despair. All I had left was a concert in London in nearly a month's time. How to kill time? Go to Switzerland? It would be too far, and it is not worth while settling in some pleasant place only for a short time. To Paris? But I have a horror of repeating the life I led there last year, and I don't want to stay there for long. Nice? That is also a long way off, and somehow I don't want to go. So in the end I have decided to stay for two or three days in Hanover and return to a normal state of mind.

Here I will write a mass of letters that are weighing me down and then move on. Maybe on the way I shall stop off in Aachen. I would again like to see the town where I was so happy and cry over the loss of Nikolai Dimitrievich. But perhaps, after all, I shall go straight to Paris. There the life of the town might kill my boredom. How much time gets lost!!!

Please embrace poor Mania for me. I kiss you and Kolia.

Yours
P. Tchaikovsky

Hanover
5-17 March 1889

Bob!

You will probably wonder why I am writing from Hanover. Quite simply, I had to write about 25 letters and have some solitude, and this is only possible in a town like Hanover where not even the stray dogs know me. Since I wrote to you last the Hamburg concert has taken place and again I must boast of a great success. The Fifth Symphony was beautifully played and I have started to love it again – I was beginning to develop an exaggerated negative opinion about it. Unfortunately, according to my correspondents, Russian papers in the Capitals continue to ignore me and apart from my nearest friends no one is interested in my successes.

On the other hand all the papers here are full of telegrams about the reception of Wagner's operas in Petersburg. I am not, of course, a Wagner; but I would, all the same, like them to know at home how well the Germans are receiving me. What do you think of the Tetralogy? I feel that we too shall soon have our own Wagnerians. I hate that species. Bored through a whole evening but suddenly struck by an impressive moment they will imagine that they have understood Wagner; and will boast about their fine appreciation, deluding both themselves and others. I do not think that Russians can like Wagner the composer of the Tetralogy (I do not mean the composer of *Lohengrin*).

These German Gods with their Valhalla quarrels and scandals, and the impossibly drawn-out dramatic nonsense, must seem merely ridiculous to the French, the Italians and the Russians. As to the music, where wonderful symphonic episodes do not save the ugliness and artificiality of the vocal side of these musical horrors, it must make you glum. But, just as in France and Italy, we shall also have our filthy breed of Wagnerites.

If all this attack on Wagner astonishes you I must tell you that I praise Wagner's creative genius very highly but I hate Wagnerism and cannot stop myself from having an aversion to his present manner...

From here Tchaikovsky travelled to Paris and then to London and then back to France from where he sailed to Constantinople. The following extract is from a letter to Modest Tchaikovsky and tells us how two great Russian composers meet fleetingly on a station platform.

TCHAIKOVSKY TO MODEST TCHAIKOVSKY

Constantinople
8 April 1889

My dear Modia!

Vassia must have told you about London. I went from London to Marseilles with terrific speed. In Paris, at the railway station, I met Kolia Rimsky-Korsakov (he wept when he saw me and I was very touched) and I travelled in the same train with the Bazilevskys. I spent only a few hours in Marseilles, from where we sailed exactly a week ago.

The steamer is very good, and the food excellent. The sea was really rough at times, and between Siros and Smyrna we had a bad storm which – even now – I can't think about without horror...

Tchaikovsky travelled extensively. The following is a letter written to Davydov from New York exactly two years later.

TCHAIKOVSKY TO VLADIMIR DAVYDOV

New York
18–30 April 1891

A minute ago I had letters from Modia, Annette, and Yurgeson. I just do not know how to say what letters mean to me in my present circumstances. I was infinitely glad.

I am keeping a diary day by day and when I return will let all of you read it – so I shall not go into details now. All I can say is that New York, American customs, American hospitality, the town itself, and the wonderful comfort of the houses, are all very much to my liking, and if I were younger I would probably have felt great pleasure in being in this interesting country. But all I do is suffer – a punishment softened somewhat by congenial circumstances. All the same all I am yearning for is home, home, home!!! There is some hope that I shall be able to leave on the 12th.

Everybody is petting, entertaining, and fussing over me, and it appears I am much better known in America than in Europe.

At first when I heard this I imagined it was only exaggerated courtesy, but now I see that this is not the case. Some of my works which are unknown in Moscow are being played here several times a season and whole articles and critical notices are written about them (e.g.. *Hamlet)*. Here I am a much more important person than in Russia. Isn't that odd?!!! The orchestral players greeted me enthusiastically at the rehearsal (so far there has only been one).

Now a few words about New York itself:

It is a huge city, not beautiful but very original. Some of the houses have only one floor, others up to eleven, and one house (a new hotel that has just been built) is seventeen storeys high. In Chicago they went even further; one of the houses there has 21 floors!!!

These high buildings are the result of New York being situated on a narrow peninsula, surrounded by water on three sides. As it cannot expand in width it has to grow in height. I have been told that in ten years time all the buildings will have at least ten floors. But out of all the arrangements in New York that would most please you, is that every apartment has a toilet room with a lavatory, bath, and wash-basin, and both the bath and the basin have constant hot and cold water. Splashing in my bath in the morning I always think of you. There is electric and gas lighting. Candles are not used at all. If one needs something one does not ask for it in the way one does in Europe – here you ring and say what you want into a tube hanging near the bell. Or if someone downstairs wants to see you, they ring you and tell you through the tube who is there and what they want. This is rather awkward for me as I do not know English. No one, except the staff, uses the stairs. The lift never stops working, running up and down at terrific speed, taking in and putting out the hotel guests.

Except for the unique way the houses in the main street alternate between being quite small or huge, what attracts your attention is that there is not much noise in the streets, nor are they very crowded. This is because there are very few cabs and horse-carriages about. The traffic consists mostly of trams, or a real railway, which has branches through the whole of this enormous city. In the morning the entire population rushes to the east – downtown – which is that part of the city where all the business premises are situated, and in the evening everyone goes uptown and home. One lives as in London, in apartments each of which has several narrow floors.

This will do for the present. Shall write soon again to one of you. I embrace you my dear, also Modest and Kolias. How much longer – oh – how much longer?

Yours
P.Tchaikovsky

A little later he wrote:

TCHAIKOVSKY TO ANATOLI TCHAIKOVSKY

To Anatoli Tchaikovsky

New York
21 April –3 May 1891

I am not going to write very much about my stay here as I shall bring back my diary which will be sent to you as soon as it has been read by the relatives in Petersburg. I am pampered, spoiled, and made a great fuss of here; but in spite of it I am homesick and apart from rare moments of solitude I am in perpetual suffering. Fortunately, however, this is not affecting my health. By the time this letter reaches you I shall have begun my return journey as I have booked on a steamer that sails on 9 – 21 May. If only this happy moment could come sooner!!! As soon as I start on my journey home a mountain will fall off my shoulders. I meet many people, see all the sights, wonder at American enterprise and the size of all their undertakings. At the rehearsals the orchestra and choir received me enthusiastically. Sometimes I do manage to have a few hours of solitude and somehow continue to carry on this miserable existence. A journey like this is not for me, or at my age! My only consolation are letters from Russia.

Thank God that Leva, the children and Nata are bearing their great loss so bravely. I kiss and embrace you all as hard as I can. From this far distance my heart burns specially brightly with love for all my dearest and nearest.

Yours
P. Tchaikovsky

Hamburg

7–19 January 1892

...Arrived the day before yesterday. Travelled in fear because Pollini insisted that I should stay with him and I hate not living in an hotel. It was lucky for me that one of his guests got stuck at his house with influenza and there was no room for me.

I spent the evening with Pollini and had supper with him. The only rehearsal took place yesterday and the performance was today. The opera had been perfectly rehearsed and quite nicely produced, but because of the changes in the recitatives which result from the use of the German text I could not help making mistakes, and in spite of everyone trying to persuade me I refused to conduct for fear of spoiling everything. Besides, the German conductor is not second-rate but quite a genius and is longing to conduct the first night. I heard him direct a wonderful performance of *Tannhäuser*.

The singers, orchestra, Pollini, stage directors, conductor (his name is Mahler), are all in love with *Eugene Onegin*; but I still wonder if the Hamburg public will be immediately attracted to it. There are quite a lot of funny things in the way it is being staged, in the costumes, sets etc.; most comic is the way in which the mazurka is danced in the third scene – this is impossible to describe. The singer who has the part of Tatiana is charming. Baritone nothing special, tenor so-so; the choruses are good, the orchestra excellent. Tomorrow evening at 11.00 I go straight to Paris to try and kill time in a pleasant way before going to Holland.

So I shall be in Paris about (I say 'about' because I am not quite sure if I will leave tomorrow) 10-22 January in the evening and I shall stay nearly two weeks, I want to try and live there incognito and work on my sextet. According to our style, on the 29th and 30th I shall conduct in Holland and leave for home on the 31st. Oh joy! Oh, happiness!

I shall write tomorrow or the day after about the first night. I embrace you uncountable times.

My address: Paris, 14 Richepanse.

Yours

P.T.

ANTONIN DVOŘÁK
1841–1904

Antonin Dvořák was born near Prague and died there aged sixty-two. He was the son of the village butcher and inn keeper and his first job was as butcher's boy. His father played the zither and Dvořák learnt the violin and also sang. In 1862 Bedřich Smetana returned to Prague to found the National Theatre of Prague. Dvořák was accepted as a viola player in the orchestra but spent much of his time composing. Later he became a church organist and gave up orchestral playing. His compositions were beginning to be played when he was befriended by Brahms who helped him to get a small State grant for poor, talented musicians. His choral music became well known in England at the various music festivals and Dvořák soon became a frequent and honoured visitor to England, much in demand as a conductor. He spent three years in New York as Head of the National Conservatory, but returned to Prague in 1895 to teach at the Conservatory there, becoming principal in 1901.

DVOŘÁK TO ANTONIN RUS DVOŘÁK

Brighton,
19 August 1885

I arrived safely on Monday, 17th August, at six-o-clock in the morning. London was still asleep. Everywhere was quiet. There was no one in the streets. I was quite tired after the journey, and on the same afternoon I had to go to Birmingham, where in the evening there was a rehearsal of the *Spectre's Bride*. It went off excellently, completely according to my wishes. The choir consisted of five hundred people, and they had rehearsed the work perfectly beforehand. Before and after the rehearsal I was received with cheers by the choir, as well as by the assembled public. On the next morning I went back to London, and to-day, as I am writing to you, I am again in another place – in the beautiful sea-coast town of Brighton, where the richest class of Londoners go in the summer. The beautiful view of the sea from my lodgings, the spectacle of the thousands of people swarming everywhere, the beautiful English women bathing here (and in public), the men and children, the vast quantity of great and small ships, then again the music playing Scottish national songs, and all kinds of other things: all this is so enchanting and fascinating that whoever has seen it will never forget it. Novello also has his beautiful house here, where I am staying, and where, thank God, I am in good health...

In October 1886, Dvořák returned to England for the fifth time to conduct the first performance of the oratorio *St. Ludmilla* in Leeds on the 15th October, followed by two performances in London. It was a great success. The enthusiasm in Victorian England for massive choral works is well shown in this letter home.

Well today it went off gloriously! The performance lasted from 12.30 p.m. to 3 p.m. All the same, no sign of weariness, not the very least. The interest kept going to the last note! I am still in the greatest state of excitement, partly the result of the remarkable performance of the orchestra (120 players), chorus (350) and soloists of the first rank; and also on account of a magnificent ovation on the part of the public. The enthusiasm – this English enthusiasm – was such as I have not experienced for a long while! I confess that I have never before been so strongly moved, nor so sensible of the flutter of excitement around me at the conductor's desk after the first and third sections. At the close of the performance I had to bow my thanks again and again in response to a tempest of applause and the calling of my name. Then I had to speak a few words of praise in English, heartily congratulating the orchestra and chorus. Again the audience broke into tempestuous applause, waved their handkerchiefs and shouted my name. I heard that at Ludmilla's aria, 'O grant me in the dust to fall,' which the famous Albani sang divinely, the public was moved to tears...

In the following letter Dvořák gives his first impressions of America to a friend in Moravia:

7 a.m., 12 October 1892

Dear Friend,

I promised to write to you and am doing so now and very gladly because when I write to the old country (as they say here) or, what is the same, to a very good friend, – being thus engaged with him – it seems to me as if I saw him here before me. And so it is today. I see you, as on a fine autumn morning, walking through the Kromeriz Park and looking sadly at the trees from which the leaves are falling one by one. But what help is there? Nature, too, needs her *diminuendo* and *morendo* so that she may come to life again and gather herself up for a great crescendo, achieving then her full strength and height in a mighty *ff.* – Where have I got to? – what am I telling you? I should be writing to you about our journey – about our crossing to America and perhaps about things concerning me personally?

Well, listen!

Our journey was lovely except for one day when everybody on board was sick except me – and so after only a short period of quarantine, we arrived safely in the promised land. The view from "Sandy Hook" (harbour town) – of New York with the magnificent Statue of Liberty (in whose head alone there is room for 60 persons and where banquets etc. are often held) – is most impressive! And then the amount of shipping from all parts of the world?! As I say amazing. On Tuesday the 27th we reached the town (Hoboken) where all ships dock, and there we were awaited by the Secretary to the National Conservatory, Mr Stanton – and what gave me special pleasure – by a Czech deputation. We exchanged greetings and a few words and then – a carriage was waiting for us and in a short time we were in New York, and are still in the same hotel. The city itself is magnificent, lovely buildings and beautiful streets and then, everywhere, the greatest cleanliness. It is dear here. Our gulden is like a dollar. At the hotel we pay 55 dollars a week for three rooms, of course in the most central part of the city, "Union Square." That does not matter, however, for we shall not spend more than 5000 and so, I am thankful to say, we shall be able to leave the rest untouched. On Sunday the 9th, there was a big Czech concert in my honour. There were 3000 people present in the hall – and there was no end to the cheering and clapping. There were speeches in Czech and English and I, poor creature, had to make a speech of thanks from the platform, holding a silver wreath in my hands. You can guess how I felt! Besides you will learn about it later from the newspapers. What the American papers write about me is simply terrible – they see in me, they say, the saviour of music and I don't know what else besides! All the scientific and political papers have been writing and are still writing about me.

I must finish as I have no more room. A hundred thousand, affectionate greetings from

A. Dvořák

1st concert at the 'Music Hall," 21st October. Te Deum, Three Overtures. Please address your letter: A.D. National Conservatory of Music 126-128. 17th Street New York, North America.

In this letter from Dvořák to his friends Mr and Mrs Hlavka in Prague he describes his life and work in America. It is interesting to note in this letter, as in others he wrote from America, how often the subject of money crops up.

Parker House, Boston
27 December 1892

Dear Sir, Esteemed Madam,

I have been wanting to write to you for a long time but have always put it off, waiting for a more suitable moment when I could tell you something of particular interest about America and especially about the musical conditions here. There is so much to tell and all so new and interesting that I cannot put it all down on paper and so I shall limit myself to the most important things.

The first and chief thing is that, thanks be to God, we are all well and liking it here very much. And why shouldn't we when it is so lovely and free here and one can live so much more peacefully – and that is what I need. I do not worry about anything and do my duty and it is all right. There are things here which one must admire and others which I would rather not see, but what can you do, everywhere there is something – in general, however, it is altogether different here, and, if America goes on like this, she will surpass all the others.

Just imagine how the Americans work in the interests of art and for the people! So, for instance, yesterday I came to Boston to conduct my obligatory concert (every thing connected with it being arranged by the highly esteemed President of our Conservatory, the tireless Mrs Jeanette M. Thurber) at which the Requiem will be given with several hundred performers. The concert on December 1st will be for only the *wealthy and the intelligentsia* but the preceding day my work will also be performed for poor workers who earn 18 dollars a week, the purpose being to give the poor and uneducated people the opportunity to hear the musical works of all times and all nations!! That's something, isn't it? I am looking forward to it like a child.

Today, Sunday, I have a rehearsal at three o'clock in the afternoon and wonder how it will come off. The orchestra here, which I heard in Brooklyn, is excellent, 100 musicians, mostly German as is also the conductor. His name is Nikisch and he comes from somewhere in Hungary. The orchestra was founded by a local millionaire, Colonel Higginson, who gave a big speech at

105

my first concert (a thing unheard of here), spoke of my coming to America and the purpose to be served by my stay here. The Americans expect great things of me and the main thing is, so they say, to show them to promised land and kingdom of a new and independent art, in short to create a national music. If the small Czech nation can have such musicians, they say, why could not they, too, when their country and people is so immense.

Forgive me for lacking a little in modesty, but I am only telling you what the American papers are constantly writing. – It is certainly both a great and splendid task for me and I hope that with God's help I shall accomplish it. There is more than enough material here and plenty of talent. I have pupils from as far away as San Francisco. They are mostly poor people, but at our Institute teaching is free of charge – anybody who is really talented pays no fees! I have only 8 pupils, but some of them are very promising.

And then not less so are the entries for the competition for prizes offered by Mrs. Thurber. 1000 dollars for an opera, 1000 for an oratory, 1000 for a libretto, 500 for a symphony, and, for a cantata, a piano or a violin concerto, 300 dollars each.

A great deal of music has come in from all over America and I must go through it all. It does not take much work. I look at the first page and can tell straight away whether it is the work of a dilettante or an artist.

As regards operas, they are very poor and I don't know whether any will be awarded a prize. Besides myself there are other gentlemen on the jury – for each kind of composition five of us. The other kinds of composition such as symphonies, concertos, suites, serenades etc. interest me very much – The composers are all much the same as at home – brought up in the German School, but here and there another spirit, other thoughts, another colouring flashes forth, in short, something Indian (something a la Bret Harte). I am very curious how things will develop. As regards my own work this is my pro-gramme: On Mondays, Wednesdays and Fridays, from 9-11, I have composi-tion; twice a week orchestra practice from 4-6 and the rest of my time is my own. You see that it is not a great deal and Mrs Thurber is very "considerate" as she wrote to me in Europe that she would be.

She looks after the administration side herself – has a secretary – also a founding member of the co-operative (very wealthy), a Mr Stanton, an inti-mate friend of Mr Cleveland, whereas Mrs. Thurber is a Republican –, but in matters of art they get on very well together and work for the good of our young and not yet fully developed institute. And so it is all right. The second secretary is Mrs MacDowel and she is mainly in charge of the correspondence.

And now something about our own domestic affairs. We live in 17th street East, 327 (only 4 mins. from the school) and are very satisfied with the flat. Mr Steinway sent me a piano immediately – a lovely one and, of course, free of charge, so that we have one nice piece of furniture in our sitting-room. Besides this we have 3 other rooms and a small room (furnished) and pay 80 dollars a month. A lot for us but the normal price here.

We have breakfast and supper at home and go to a boarding-house for dinner.

I must stop. My kind regards to yourself and your wife,

I remain, Gratefully Yours,

Antonin Dvořák

My wife, who is with me, asks to be remembered to you.

CHARLES VILLIERS STANFORD
1852-1924

Stanford was an Irish Protestant and had little time for the Catholic theology of Elgar's *The Dream of Gerontius* with its words by Cardinal Newman. He was to make the oft-quoted remark that 'it stinks of incense'. However, in the following letter he supports the piece, showing his fair-mindedness and recognition of an important and inspired work.

CHARLES VILLIERS STANFORD TO J.H. GREEN

15 March 1902

When I say this (about the failure to consult him about works to be performed; not confined, apparently, to the Festival Committee) I say so especially with regard to the apparently curt dismissal of Elgar's Dream of Gerontius.

A work which is the first English composition to be given at a Lower Rhine Festival *is not a work to be simply dismissed because A or B don't personally care for it*. It is the duty of a great choral society in a great town to let its public form their own judgement on such an important composition which has even reached with success in Germany in its most Anglophobic temper. It is this spirit of private prejudices overriding public duties which has been at the root of the difficulties which so many composers have had during their lives. Look at Berlioz! Fancy a Philharmonic Committee in the '60's voting a performance of Faust! I can hear the easy way in which it would have been ruled out of Court. Surely it is for a choral society such as yours to lead and not to follow.

LEOS JANÁČEK
1854-1928

Leos Janáček was born the son of a village schoolmaster in Moravia, on the border of Moravia and Silesia. This was an area which he always regarded as 'home'. At ten he became a choirboy at Brno where he was strongly influenced by monastic music. He then studied in Prague and later at Leipzig. When he was nearly thirty he settled back in Brno where he became conductor, teacher, student of folk music and composer. As well as being a composer of the operas *Jenufa* and *The Cunning Little Vixen*, he also composed orchestral and choral music and passionate chamber music. This was inspired by Kamila Stosslova, with whom he fell in love at the age of sixty-three in 1917. He wrote to her almost every day. Nothing expressed his love for her so much as his second string quartet written in a couple of weeks, a few months before he died. He first called the quartet *Love Letters* but was later to change it to *Intimate Letters*.

JANÁČEK TO KAMILA STOSSLOVA

Brno
1st February 1928

At night
My dear Kamila!
I came to my post box, saw your letter lying there – and gasped with joy! I am now writing before opening your letter. I know that without you my life would be a parched meadow. At each step I would say, there a flower once blossomed, here another – and there would be sadness to choking point. Now I shall read your letter! I think that it will give me pleasure – if only because you have written!...

Tell me truthfully whether you have a cough, whether you have a pain in the back, either aching or stabbing. If so, you will have to look for a spa cure as soon as Spring comes. I am glad that you have forgiven me. My letters, I know, have turned bitter. Now it will be different.

I have now begun to write something nice. Our life will be in it. It'll be called *"Love letters"*.

I think it's going to sound delightful. After all, those pleasant experiences of ours have already been plentiful enough! Like little fires in my soul, they will light up into the most beautiful melodies.

Just imagine! I finished the first movement in Hukvaldy. That impression on seeing you for the first time!

Now I am working on the second movement; I think it will dawn on that hot < * > in Luhacovice. In particular the whole work will be held together by a special instrument. It's called the *viola d'amour* – the viola of love. Oh, how I am looking forward to it! In this work I shall always be alone with you! No third person beside us. Full of longings as if with you there in that heaven of ours. How I shall enjoy working on it. After all, you must know that, apart from you, I know no other world! You are everything to me, I want nothing else but your love.

And how bitter I was when I read in your letter how you would like to forget everything beautiful that has passed between us! I was thinking, is it possible that my Kamila can forget it all? Could it be possible? Now I know that it wouldn't! In our heaven we have reached that point where it's no longer possible to go back, only upwards! Draw strength from this; you are certain to find peace. If I am somebody and my works count, then it follows that *you are also somebody – and higher and more important* than that ordinary niece of mine, who will never be allowed to stand in my presence again. That's how it is, my dear Kamilka! Don't blame your nerves for everything; that bronchitis has put you into a terrible mood. It'll also pass.

And don't be ashamed of your nature. It's so dear, so very dear to me. You are laughter "mixed" from tears. It is that nature – I understand it quite a lot already – which is almost chronically sensitive. You are difficult to understand. What surrounds you is hard – and, Kamilka, heartless. It's better to avoid hard stones than to fall among them.

So, my precious Kamilka, keep writing; if it's only two or three words it'll satisfy me.

*A word was scratched out on the original letter.

And were you to write "I am forever yours", you would open heaven for me!...

Forever yours

L.

Brno

8th February, 1928

At night

My dear Kamila,

You have no idea what impression your letter from yesterday made on me! To wake up at night and not sleep till morning! In my head, a whirl of thoughts! How will you answer me tomorrow? Will you again avoid speaking directly? After all, you do know how to speak from the heart!...

Today I wrote down in music that sweetest longing of mine. I wrestle with it, it's winning through. You are giving birth. What deal in life would that little son of ours have? What would be your lot? Just like you sinking from tears into laughter, that's how it sounds.

Now I am just waiting for your reply. What will you do, so that it can never be gone back on?! Be it as it may. I have never known what it is to look back. What's done is done! Come the new day, a new sun! That's you! For some it always comes out; for others it remains behind the clouds. I am not forcing you to anything. I shall be waiting devotedly, with complete trust. I shall fight my way through those clouds and – perhaps you shall be mine! It would be a strange fate – to fight for our one and only happiness and not achieve it! I need to have you close to me; that means Spring. Otherwise I become gloomy. Today I feel like that. Until you answer me how it'll be so that there is no going back! I shall grasp that letter as if it were fate.

Forever yours,

L.

Your letter led me into seventh heaven. May I remain there and you with me!

110

At night

My dear Kamilka!

Today I succeeded with that movement "when the earth trembled". It'll be the best. After all, it was amazingly beautiful! And it was truthful. Only the best melodies could be attached to it. Now there is the final movement to be accomplished. It will be like anxiety for you. You know, such anxiety, that I would tie you up as I would little legs of a lambkin, so it wouldn't wander.

Today I am so depressed after work – and no refreshment! Sadness in my soul.

I know that you are as sensitive as I am. I think that if I now have some silent pain, you also will feel it. And it would be good if we were only to laugh. We can cover up a lot with laughter. And don't burn this letter. It will be just as well for people to know one day that our lives, just like anyone else's, have a rough and a smooth side. I have only that rough side. I need you to stroke it! –

Forever yours,

L.

FROM KAMILA STOSSLOVA TO JANÁČEK

Pisek
14th March 1928

Dear Maestro,

I have been reading your letters many times over, they are nice and make me think of you even if I didn't want to. I am so glad about being alone here that I can't describe it to you. I go to bed at 7 o'clock every day. And the peace is the same as you have. While reading today's letter from you, I am thinking about all that has happened and about all our experiences, and I am happy. You make me think like this when you describe how your life used to be and how it is now. As for mine, I didn't know anything and didn't long for anything. And so it went by without any love and happiness. I went along thinking that that was how it was meant to be.

I now think that God has been testing you and me and when he saw that we were good and that we deserve it, he has granted us this joy in life. If I were to tell anyone that for the whole of my life I could find no one who would offer me his love and that perhaps I had been waiting for you, they would not believe me. All this I have tried to avoid and I have not sought any-thing – you alone, who have known me all these years, know this to be indeed true. Some people may doubt that it is possible; yes, it is possible for you to be dearer to me than if you were a young man.

I assure you that my life is an enjoyable one and that I wouldn't wish for anything better. And you alone are guilty of that. I must also thank you for it...

FROM JANÁČEK TO KAMILA STOSSLOVA

Brno
18th May, 1928

At night
My dear Kamila,
...Today, at 3 o'clock, the Moravian Quartet are coming to my house to play my / your composition! I am keen to hear it...

So they played the first and the third movements! And, Kamila, it's going to be a beautiful, special, boisterous, inspired composition, beyond all conven-tion! Together we shall win through! It is my first composition to spring from directly experienced emotion. Previously, my compositions have been based only on memories; this work, *Intimate letters*, has been composed in a fire. The previous compositions only in hot ashes.

This work will be dedicated to you; you are the cause of it and composing it has been my greatest pleasure.

I am asking Prof. Vymetal to invite the Moravian Quartet to perform it in Pisek in the Autumn...When it goes all round the world, we shall rejoice together...

Forever yours,
L.

EDWARD ELGAR
1857-1943

Elgar was born at Broadheath near Worcester. His family were musical. His father was an organist and music seller. Edward grew up playing many instruments: violin, cello, double-bass, piano, bassoon and trombone. As a young man he earned his living by becoming a professional violinist and a music teacher. The Three Choirs Festival had established itself nearby in Worcester and Elgar became very involved in it, playing in the Festival Orchestra. Gradually, however, he became known for his composing. A quintessentially English composer, his reputation was firmly established in 1899 with his *Enigma Variations* – a collection of musical portraits of his friends. Many of his compositions were seen as patriotic and imperialist, epitomised in *Land of Hope and Glory*. He was painfully honest, a Roman Catholic, and his *Dream of Gerontius* is a towering testament to his faith. Elgar was enormously helped and stimulated by the company of women, in particular his wife Alice.

He became great friends with Dr C.W. Buck of Giggleswick, Yorkshire who was an amateur musician, cellist and conductor. During their long friendship they exchanged many letters and visits. Elgar appeared to be very affected by adverse comments of the critics and relied upon the support of friends such as Dr Buck.

The following is a letter to him written shortly after the first performance of an early work, *Intermezzo Mauresque*.

ELGAR TO DR BUCK

4 Field Terrace, Worcester.

Jany. 14, 1884

My dear Doctor,

If not too late – a happy new year and many of them. I have been loath to write before, for I have had nothing worth telling you. I had a good success at Birm. despite what the papers say; the man who wrote the slighting article is a Mus. Bac. who had sent in two pieces and they were advertised and withdrawn because the orchestration wanted so much revision as to be unplayable! Enough of this – I had a characteristic letter from Pollitzer – he asked for the parts and is trying to introduce the sketch in London – I don't anticipate a performance tho' I will let you know if it comes off.

I was sorely disappointed at not going to town – But 'tis no use going there to sit in the house all day – well – I have no money – not a cent. And I am sorry to say have no prospects of getting any.

We have had a very quiet time; my father was ill just before Xmas which made it dismal; the younger generation at the Catholic Ch: have taken an objection to him and have got him turned out of the Organist's place; this he had held for 37 years!! He thinks a great deal of this and I fear 'twill break him up. Frank gets on: was playing 2nd to Horton at Birmingham on Dec. 26. and it seems to me that the only person who is an utter failure in this miserable world is myself.

I have heard from Arthur and was glad he is going to Leipzig. I fancy he will get good lessons, there are few, comparatively, for the 'cello.

What have you gone and done? He says 'the Doctor is in great glee over this last business!' Surely 'tis not matrimony; I am more than anxious to know all about it. I suppose I begin regular work next week, but I don't look forward to it. I am disappointed, disheartened and sick of this world altogether.

I hope you had a good time in town, did you get any music? I thought much about you and wondered how the trios went.

What a business about Barrett! I saw he was garotted but have heard nothing since. Well – 'tis time I was retiring– I am afraid I have sent you a dismal epistle – sorry for it – better next time.

Will you please give my kind regards to Mrs Buck and all I know .

& with best wishes, I am, my dear doctor,
Always sincerely yours
Edward Elgar

P.S. Miss Weaver is remaining in Worcester and the little Music etc that we get together is the only enjoyment I get and more than I deserve no doubt.

> Elgar was spending a good deal of time in Malvern and one of the most exciting events of these years was when Dvorak visited Worcester and the Three Choirs Festival to conduct his *Stabat Mater* and *Symphony in D Major*. Elgar was playing in the orchestra and was very inspired. He wrote to Dr Buck, 'I wish you could hear Dvorak's music. It is simply ravishing, so tuneful and clever and the orchestration is wonderful: no matter how few instruments he uses it never sounds thin. I cannot describe it; it must be heard.'
> Despite his increasing reputation and demand as a solo violinist within the county, Elgar was pessimistic. 'My prospects,' he wrote to Dr Buck, 'are about as hopeless as ever. I am not wanting in energy I think; so,

ELGAR TO FRANK SCHUSTER

Severn House
August 25th

My Dear Frank:

I don't know where you are so I send this home. I hope you are well & getting some clean & clear air. Here we are very hot but atmosphere quite bearable. London looks normal; it seems incredible that things shd. go on so well. Alice is well but worried...I am a s.constable & am a "Staff Inspector." I am sure others cd. do the work better but none with a better will. I was equipping (serving out "weapons"), & taking receipts & registering my men for hours last night: this morning at six I inspected the whole district – so one does what one can – its a pity I am too old to be a soldier. I am so active.

Everything is at a standstill & we have nothing left in the world – absolute financial ruin – but we are cheerful & I will die a man if not a musician.

That is all about us & now about you? do write. Concerning the war I say nothing – the only thing that wrings my heart & soul is the thought of the horses – oh! my beloved animals – the men – and women can go to hell – but my horses; I walk round & round this room cursing God for allowing dumb beasts to be tortured – let Him kill his human beings but – how CAN HE? Oh my horses.

Bless you
Yrs. ever affcly.
Edward

Concerts continued during the war, though as far as possible excluding German music. This was particularly difficult as Elgar owed a great debt to the German musical tradition.

On April 6th 1920 Lady Elgar died. It was a bitter blow to Elgar and once more he turned to his long-standing friends for support.

ELGAR TO FRANK SCHUSTER

Kirkland
Little Malvern,
Monday April 12

My Dearest Frank,

We have had a real rest. This is the quietest place ever known & we are the only people here – we can see the little grave in the distance & nothing cd. be sweeter & lovelier only birds singing & all *remote* peace brought closely to us. I cannot thank you enough for the quartet – it was exactly right & just what she wd. have loved – but once more you must please let me settle the acct when you know what it is: the boys played like angels.

As to our future we know nothing: Carice will stay here with friends & I shall lead a normal sort of life – at my sister's & round about until business calls me home.

I hope the day was not too tiring for you & once more heartfelt thanks. The place she chose long years ago is too sweeet – the blossoms are white all round it & the illimitable plain, with all the hills & churches in the distance which were hers from childhood, looks just the same – inscrutable & unchanging. If it has to be – it could not be better.

The words do not quite suit but all the time the line from In Memoriam comes to me – "I think my friend is richly shrined" – & thank you for making the last plaintive little scene something far away from the commonplace.

Ever your friend
Edward

ELGAR TO TROYTE GRIFFITH

The Elms Stoke Prior
Bromsgrove.
Ap. 19 1920

Dear Troyte:

I do not know how I shd. have got through the awfully lonely time without your friendship & care. As the days go by – (I am, with Carice, at my sister's) – the "blank" seems greater and unbearable.

I wish you would see if the *next space* to the little lonely grave is to be had & if so secure it for me: I shd. like to know this at once & shd. be glad if you wd. have a simple (enclosing) edging of stone put round the graves or the grave & unoccupied space – if the latter is secured.

Carice & I send our love to you.

Yours ever
Edward Elgar

After his wife's death Elgar had not the inclination to compose a great deal but he fully participated in the musical life of London.

In 1922 he welcomed Richard Strauss to London.

12 June 1922

Dear Dr Richard Strauss,

I send you a word of warm welcome & an assurance that your return to our country gives the greatest pleasure to myself & to very many of my musical countrymen.

I hope we may meet soon. With cordial greetings.

Believe me to be
Your sincere friend
Edward Elgar

This was the reply:

My Very Dear Friend,

I thank you heartily for your dear letter with its renewed expression of your sympathy and kindly feeling – always so precious to me.

Unhappily my son is ill, and I cannot leave the hotel, within the next few days, except with difficulty.

Will you be good enough to tell me when and where I may see you? Convey my sincere compliments to your wife also.

I remain
Your ever devoted admirer
Richard Strauss

Shortly afterwards, accompanied by Bernard Shaw, Elgar entertained Strauss to lunch at the United Services Club.

Arnold Bax and Arthur Bliss both wrote to Elgar, grateful for his help and encouragement.

ARTHUR BLISS TO ELGAR

21, Holland Park, London
Dec. 26 (1920)

Dear Sir Edward,

I thought I should like to write and wish you the best of health and happiness for 1921, and also to thank you so much for giving me the chance of writing a work* for the Gloucester Festival. It is a great opportunity, and I look on it as one more proof of your generosity to us younger musicians.

*Colour Symphony

I do not think you realise what a fine and rare encouragement your presence is, when as you did at luncheon the other day you gave the lead to younger composers. It is such a unique thing, this broadminded generosity, that I hope you will be long spared to make the music of Englishmen preeminent.

Yours ever
Arthur Bliss

BAX TO ELGAR

155 Fellows Rd N.W.3
March 3, 1921

Dear Sir Edward,

I hope you will not mind if I give myself the pleasure of dedicating to you a string quartet* of mine that is now in the press. I think I may say that I have always been one of the warmest admirers of your work, and beyond this I have never forgotten a wonderful day of summer twenty years ago when George Alder brought me to see you at "Birchwood." I was only seventeen then and much has happened since, but I should be very pleased if you will accept this simple work in memory of an unforgettable day and all the pleasure your own music has given me.

Yours very sincerely,
Arnold Bax

However encouraging Elgar was to the young, he felt increasingly left behind, restless and disillusioned. He was 67 years of age.

ELGAR TO FRANK SCHUSTER

Napleton Grange
November 15

My dear Frank

Thank you for your letter from Paris. It was very sad over Faure's death – he was such a real gentleman – the highest type of Frenchman & I admire him greatly. His chamber music never had a chance here in the old Joachim days I fear; I may be wrong but I feel that it was 'held up' to our loss...

*String Quartet No. 1 in G

...and later:

Dec. 30 1924

Dear Frank,

I had a very quiet time only Troyte here & a dog or two. I fear you will have nothing more from "my pen" – but if that's all to look forward to you will not miss much: music is dying fast in this country.

Thank you – but I do not intend to stray far & the S. Coast [this in reply to an invitation to Brighton where Schuster was now living] will not see me again. Yes, the weather has been wonderful & I find I have driven 1500 miles about this dear old county in six weeks. I thought the notice of Puccini [died November 29] dreadfully inadequate.

Yrs ever
Edward Elgar

GIACOMO PUCCINI
1858-1924

Puccini was born in Lucca in Tuscany, Italy and was the fifth generation of a family of professional musicians holding official positions in Italy. He trained at the Milan Conservatory. His first opera to be performed was *Le Villi* when he was twenty six. Thereafter there was a steady output of works.

Bernard Shaw, in his capacity as music critic, said of him, 'Puccini looks to me more like the heir of Verdi than any of his rivals.'

The following letters show how he worked with his librettist. He is constantly exchanging correspondence containing scores. In one letter he writes 'O you of the city, think to more purpose of one who is waiting in the country! I need not only the first act, but the third also, since then Act II would be finished.' He is talking about what was to be his last opera, *Turandot*...

Before it was completed he died in Brussels of cancer of the throat, aged sixty five.

PUCCINI TO GIUSEPPE ADAMI, A LIBRETTIST

May 15, 1920

Dear Adamino,

Turandot! Act I – very good! I like the *mise en scene* too. The three masks are very successful. I am not quite sure about the effectiveness of the close, but I may be wrong. The truth is that it is a good act and well laid out. What will the second act be like? Shall we need the third? Or will the action be exhausted in the second? Go ahead with it, using all your imagination and resourcefulness, and the opera will be not only original but *moving*. And it is on this last that I lay most stress, and this we must achieve. Good Beppino and Renato! Thank you! I go to London on Tuesday for eight or ten days. I beg you to get on with the work, so that I may as soon as possible get an idea of the whole thing.

Affectionately yours

Torre del Lago
July 18, 1920

Dear Adami,

Your packet to hand. At first sight it seems to me good, except for some criticisms which I might make in both the second and third acts. In the third – I had imagined a different *denouement* – I had thought that her capitulation would be more *prenante*, and I should have liked her to burst into expressions of love *coram populo* – but excessively, violently, shamelessly, like a bomb exploding.

We must meet. Will Renato come to Bagni di Lucca? Will you? You will understand that I don't want to come and roast in Milan, but it would be convenient (I mean it is urgent) to meet as soon as possible. We've got our canvas, a large one, and an original and perhaps unique work. But it needs some alterations, which we shall devise when we meet to discuss it.

All my affectionate regards to you and Renato.

In the following letter Puccini is anxiously awaiting the score of his next piece, *La Rondine*. In another letter he says, 'It is urgent because it has forty theatres waiting.'

Torre del Lago
December 3, 1920

Dear Adamino,

On Saturday I hope to leave for the Maremma. As soon as I have settled in there I shall write, or, better, wire to you to come. Then please let me know in good time, a few days before. Try to arrive by the morning train or in the evening by the one due at some thing after six: *consult the timetable*. Your station is Orbetello, and from there to the jungle it is about five miles – by infernal roads – but when you are there it is either suicide or bliss unalloyed. There is no middle way. Well, that is settled. Bring me the orchestra score of *La Rondine*, first edition, and some copies of the libretto. I have the piano arrangement here. It will be better if you send a telegram too. Send it to Orbetello, just two days before you are coming.

Yours affectionately...

PUCCINI TO ARTURO TOSCANINI THE CONDUCTOR

Milan
2 February 1923

Dear Arturo,

You have given me the greatest satisfaction of my life.

In your wonderful interpretation *Manon* became a far better work than I had thought in those far-off days—you performed this music of mine with such poetic feeling, such *souplesse* and irresistible passion.

Last night I truly felt the greatness of your soul and all your affection for your old friend and companion of those early struggles.

I am happy because you showed, above all, such an understanding for the spirit of my passionate youth of thirty years ago! My beloved creature in hands of Arturo Toscanini! I thank you from the depth of my heart!

CLAUDE ACHILLE DEBUSSY
1862–1918

Debussy was born near Paris to poor parents, He was the founder of what has been called the Impressionist School in music, echoing the great painters of the time such as Monet. As a young man he was in fact very influenced by Wagner but with the encouragement of other French composers such as Satie, he strove to find a French voice.

He attended the Paris Conservatoire from the age of twelve. When he was eighteen he met Baroness von Meck the wealthy patron of Tchaikovsky. She was enormously interested in Debussy and wrote to Tchaikovsky of her faith in him, despite the fact that she felt he played with no feeling.

125

BARONESS VON MECK TO TCHAIKOVSKY

Interlaken, 17 August 1880

Yesterday for the first time I played our Symphony with my little Frenchman. So to-day I am in a terrible state of nerves. I cannot play it without a fever penetrating all the fibres of my being and for a whole day I cannot recover from the impression. My partner did not play it well, though he read it splendidly. That is his only, though very important merit. He reads a score, even yours, à livre ouvert. He has another merit, which is that he is delighted with your music...

He does not care for the Germans and says: 'Ils ne sont pas de notre tempérament, ils sont si lourds, pas clairs.' On the whole he is a typical Parisian boulevard product. It seems he is eighteen and has already graduated at the Conservatoire avec premier prix. Blessed are those who study at the Paris Conservatoire. He composes nicely, but there he is the true Frenchman...

> However, he won the Prix de Rome which entitled him to three years' study there. This he undertook unwillingly only lasting out for two. On his return to Paris he was to compose the *Prélude à L'Après Midi d'un Faune, Pelléas et Mélisande* and much more.

DEBUSSY TO M VASNIER

Rome,
February 1885

...Here I am in this abominable villa. I can tell you that my first impressions are not very favourable. It's awful weather – rainy and windy. There was no need to come to Rome to have the same weather as Paris, especially for one with such a grudge against Rome as I have.

My friends came to meet me at Monte Rotondo, where six of us slept in one dirty little room. If only you knew how changed I am! None of their good-hearted friendly ways of Paris. They're stiff and impressed with their own importance – too much Prix de Rome about them.

In the evening when I arrived at the Villa I played my cantata, which was well received by some, but not by all the musicians.

I don't mind. The artistic atmosphere and cameraderie that we are told about seem to me to be very exaggerated. With one or two exceptions, it is difficult to talk to people here, and when I hear their ordinary conversation I cannot help thinking of the fine talks we used to have which opened my mind to so many things. Then the people here are so egoistic. I've heard the musicians demolishing each other – Mart and Pierné against Vidal, Pierné and Vidal against Marty, and so on.

Ah! When I got back to my enormous room, where you have to walk a league from one piece of furniture to the another, I felt so lonely that I cried! I'm so used to your friendship and to your asking me about my work. I shall never forget all you have done for me and the place I had in your family. I shall do all I can to prove to you that I am not ungrateful. So please don't forget me, for I feel I am going to need you.

I've tried to work but I can't. You know how much I love music and how much this state of mind annoys me. This is not the life for me. Their happiness isn't mine. It's not pride that makes me hate this life. I can't get used to it. I have no feeling for it and haven't the necessary indifference.

Yes, I fear that I shall have to return to Paris earlier than you think. It may appear silly, but what do I do? I don't want to make you cross and I should be very sorry to try your friendship. But whatever you think, you can't accuse me of lacking courage, I'm rather unwell – Rome again – my beastly heart doesn't seem to be working properly. I rack my brain to work, but nothing comes of it except a fever which knocks me down completely.

I was so pleased to get your letter, and if I'm not asking too much, I know how little time you have, send me a long letter to remind me of the pleasant talks we used to have.

Very affectionately.
Your devoted
ACH. DEBUSSY

Early in 1887 Debussy decided to leave Rome after only two years instead of the required three. As he explained to M. Vasnier:

You know how doubtful I am of myself. When something of mine pleased you it gave me courage. Here I should never have that. My friends make fun of my sadness and I should never get any encouragement from them. If things don't go better I know that many people will give me up. But I'd rather do twice as much work in Paris than drag out this life here…

DEBUSSY TO ERNEST CHAUSSON

Paris,
6 September 1893

...Here I am, just turned thirty-one and not quite sure of my aesthetic. There are still things that I am not able to do – create masterpieces for instance, or be really responsible – for I have the fault of thinking too much about myself and only seeing reality when it is forced upon me and then being insurmountable. Perhaps I am rather to be pitied than blamed. In any case I am writing you this expecting your pardon and your patience.

> Chausson replied that 'in his opinion Debussy knew perfectly well what he wanted'.
> In the summer of 1892 Debussy bought a copy of the newly published *Pelléas and Mélisande* by Maeterlinck and he began to consider setting some of its scenes to music. After seeing the play the next year he decided to use it as the text for an opera, a task that was to take him nine years.

DEBUSSY TO ERNEST CHAUSSON

January 1894

Dear Friend,

It's Mélisande's fault – so will you forgive us both? I have spent days in pursuit of those fancies of which she is made. I had no courage to tell you of it all – besides, you know what such struggles are. I don't know if you have never gone to bed, as I have, with a strange desire to cry, feeling as if you had not been able to see during the day some greatly loved friend. Just now I am worried about Arkel. He is from the other side of the grave and has that fond love, disinterested and far-seeing, of those who will soon disappear – all of which has to be said with *do ré mi fa sol la si do*. What a job!

I shall write to you at greater length to-morrow. This is just for you to know that I am thinking of you and to wish you good day.

> In 1885 the first version of *Pelléas and Mélisande* was finished. Following an unsuccessful attempt to have it produced at the Théâtre de la Monnaie in Brussels it was suggested by Ysaÿe that Debussy present a concert performance of selected sections. Debussy would not agree.

13 October 1896

Dear Great Friend

I was most touched by your kind letter and your friendly anxiety for *Pelléas and Mélisande*. The poor little creatures are so difficult to introduce into the world, for with a godfather like you the world doesn't want to have anything to do with them.

Now I must humbly tell you why I am not of your opinion about a performance of *Pelléas in part*. Firstly, if this work has any merit, it is the connection between the drama and the music. It is quite obvious that at a concert performance this connection would disappear and no one could be blamed for seeing nothing in those eloquent 'silences' with which this work is starred. Moreover, as the simplicity of the work only gains significance on the stage, at a concert performance they would throw in your face the American wealth of Wagner and I'd be like some poor fellow who couldn't afford to pay for 'contra-bass tubas'! In my opinion *Pelléas and Mélisande* must be given *as they are*, and then it will be a matter of taking them or leaving them, and if we have to fight, it will be worth while.

> Amongst other contemporary French poets Mallarmé provided inspiration and the eclogue for *Prélude à l'Après-midi d'un faune*. These were Debussy's impressions upon listening to it, as recounted to G. Jean-Aubry in a letter.

25th March 1910

I used to live then in a little furnished flat in the rue de Londres…Mallarmé came in with his prophetic air and his Scotch plaid around him. After listening to it he remained silent for a long time; then said: 'I didn't expect anything like that. This music draws out the emotion of my poem and gives it a warmer background than colour.' And here are the lines that Mallarmé wrote on a copy of *L'Après-midi d'un faune* which he sent me after the first performance:

> 'Sylvain d'haleine première,
> Si ta flûte a réussi
> Ouïs toute la lumiere
> Qu'y soufflera Debussy.'

Gradually Debussy was changing the face of French music and, though normally modest and disciplined, he let rip at times when presented with a work which he felt in his heart to be inferior. Thus he wrote to Pierre Louÿs about Charpentier's successful opera *Louise:*

DEBUSSY TO PIERRE LOÜYS

5th February 1900

Dear Pierre,

I have been to the show of the Charpentier family, so that I am in just the right state of mind to appreciate the forcefulness of your letter. It seems to me that this work had to be. It supplies only too well the need for that cheap beauty and idiotic art that has such an appeal. You see what this Charpentier has done. He has taken the cries of Paris which are so delightfully human and picturesque and, like a rotten 'Prix de Rome,' he has turned them into sickly cantilenas with harmonies underneath that, to be polite, we will call parasitic. The sly dog! It's a thousand times more conventional than *Les Huguenots,* of which the technique, although it may not appear so, is the same. And they call this Life. Good God! I'd sooner die straight away. What you have here is something of the feeling after the twentieth half-pint, and the sloppiness of the chap who comes back at four in the morning, falling all over the crossing-sweeper and the rag-and-bone man. And this man imagines he can express the soul of the poor!!! It's so silly that it's pitiful.

Of course M. Mendès discovers his Wagner in it and M. Bruneau his Zola. And they call this a real French work! There's something wrong somewhere. It's more silly than harmful. But then people don't very much like things that are beautiful – they are so far from their nasty little minds. With many more works like *Louise* any attempt to drag them out of the mud will completely fail.

I assure you that I'd very much like *Pelléas* to be played in Japan, for our fashionable eclectics might approve of it – and I can tell you that I should be ashamed.

Thank you for your kind and lovely letter, and a bièntôt, eh?

Your Claude.

In the summer of 1904 Debussy's life was fraught with scandal. He left his second wife, Lily Texier, for a rich woman, Madame Emma Bardac, whereupon Lily shot herself and was taken to a nursing home. Debussy lost several of his friends over the affair but in the autumn of 1905 the couple had a baby girl. They were married some time later.

He wrote to a new friend, the critic Louis Laloy:

April 1905

You should know how people have deserted me! It is enough to make one sick of every one called a man. I shan't tell you of all that I have gone through. It's ugly and tragic and ironically reminds one of a novel a concierge might read. Morally I have suffered terribly. Have I some forgotten debt to pay to life? I don't know; but often I've had to smile so that no one should see that I was going to cry. So, my dear friend, be assured of my joy on seeing you again. I shall try to bring up the old Claude Debussy you knew. If he is rather care-ridden don't mind, for his affection for you is unshaken.

Grand Hotel
Eastbourne
28th August, 1905

It would have been unpardonable to leave Paris without seeing you if my departure had not been a flight. I fled from all that tedious fuss. I fled from myself, who was finally only allowed to think by permission of the usher. I've been here a month. It's a little English seaside place, silly as these places sometimes are. I shall have to go because there are too many draughts and too much music – but I don't quite know where…I am trying somehow to get back to myself. I have written a certain amount of music as I have not done for quite a time.

By the time war broke out in 1914 Debussy was battling against poor physical health.

8th August 1914

My dear Jacques,

Your letter has reassured me and I am really glad to have got your news.

You know that I have no *sang-froid* and certainly nothing of the army spirit. I've never had a rifle in my hands. My recollections of 1870 and the anxiety of my wife, whose son and son-in-law are in the army, prevent me from becoming very enthusiastic.

All this makes my life intense and troubled. I am just a poor little atom crushed in this terrible cataclysm. What I am doing seems so wretchedly small. I've got to the state of envying Satie who, as a corporal, is really going to defend Paris.

And so, my dear Jacques, if you have any work that you can give me, do not forget me. Forgive me for counting on you, but you are really all I have.

Your devoted,

C.D.

October 1915

I am enjoying these last days of liberty. I think of Paris as a sort of prison where one has not even the right to think and where even the walls have ears...I am writing down all the music that comes into my head – like a madman, and rather sadly too. Now the curtains have gone from the windows and when I see a trunk it makes me feel as sad as a cat...

Paris,

8th June 1916

The sick man again thanks you for your friendly inquiries. As the days go by I must admit that I am losing patience. I have been tried too long. I wonder whether this illness isn't incurable? I might as well be told at once. 'Alor! Oh! Alors!' as poor Golaud cries.

Life has become too hard, and Claude Debussy, writing no more music, has no longer any reason to exist. I have no hobbies. They never taught me anything but music. That wouldn't matter if I wrote a great deal; but to tap on an empty head is disrespectful.

On 5th May 1917 he appeared on the concert platform in Paris for the last time. With Gaston Poulet he played the piano and violin *Sonata*. From the beginning of 1918 he was confined to his house. His cancer was incurable. The bombardment of Paris began on 23rd March and he heard the noise of the shells exploding in the streets as he died on Monday 25th March 1918.

FREDERICK DELIUS
1862–1934

Delius was born in Bradford of German and Dutch ancestry. His family were wool traders and although he showed an early gift for music, he began training for the family business. However, his business travels abroad only served to develop further his passion for music. He became a full-time composer and in 1897 he married and settled in France, where he remained for the rest of his life.

He became great friends with Grieg and Grainger and the three of them corresponded regularly. He wrote this letter to Grieg whilst staying in his uncle Theodor's apartment near the Paris Opera where he enjoyed meeting many of his uncle's artistic friends.

DELIUS TO EDVARD GRIEG

43 Rue Cambon
Paris
(mid-May 1888)

Dear Grieg,

I have now settled down a bit & must confess that I feel very happy here. There is something in the atmosphere that is quite different from Germany or England. The hustle & bustle here is extraordinary, one is bound to think that every street urchin enjoys life. The concerts are over. I heard the last Lamoureux Concert & must confess that as far as ensemble & finesse are concerned the orchestra is far superior to Leipzig. I heard Parsifal Prelude, Tannhauser Overture, Lohengrin Prelude to 1st Act, Women's March & Prelude to 3rd Act, Dance Marcabre Saint Saens, L'Arlesienne, Bizet & something from Bizet's opera The Pearl Fishers, quite excellent. I am meeting a lot of artists, musicians & writers. But I can't do much work. In a few weeks' time I am going to Spain, Seville or Granada, am already longing for it.* It is beautiful, very beautiful here but I will soon have to have some peace & quiet. I heard a new opera by Lalo at the Opera Comique, but found it utterly trivial. Also Aida at the big Opera, quite excellent. How did your concert come off, did it bring in pounds stirling en masse for you. I have not heard anything from Sinding nor from Mr Braun. The weather is quite marvellous, not a cloud. My kind regards to your wife. I hope that you are both keeping well &

*This proposed trip to Spain was not to be realized

133

happy. Please excuse this superficial letter, as soon as I have some peace you shall receive a much more detailed one.

Farewell & write me a few lines.

Your devoted

Fritz Delius

43 Rue Cambon

Paris.

June 20/88

My good, dear Grieg,

How are you, where are you? What are you doing? & how did you get on in London? You have no idea how much I miss you & have missed you since not seeing you any more. This evening I felt that I just wanted to say it to you. Yes! I think of you very often. I have been all alone here for the past 18 days. My uncle was in London & has only just come back today. I have been working the whole time & have written a lot, several songs, and Ibsen's *Paa Viddern,* for tenor voice, & an orchestral piece. For you I have written two songs in remembrance which I should like to send as soon as I know your correct address. Next year I am certainly coming to Trollhaugen, if I am alive. Give my greetings to the North, until I am able to do so myself. It is very beautiful in Paris, but I would not like to stay here for ever. The French are very artistic, but it is always merely art, the great vitality of Nature is missing, at least in music. It is all too refined & affected – But one can learn much, very much here. The people are very free & have power, & everyone lives & is free: a great contrast to Germany. Moral freedom is widespread here too. In a few weeks' time I travel to Spain, Seville first. I will write & tell you all about it. From time to time I go to the Morgue where people who have died are laid out, suicides, or murdered. Oh, it's saddening to go in there. There are always 4 or 5 pitiful corpses looking so eternally wretched. Yes, you can very soon come across the two extremes here. The people of luxury in their fine carriages in the Bois de Boulogne & the miserable suicides in the Morgue. If only I had *you* here I could show you so very much. Things you could weep over, but also other things which would amuse you a lot. Now & again I also go where the very poorest people live. I dress shabbily & then go everywhere undisturbed.

You can see 5 different worlds here in Paris, it is immensely interesting. If you have time write me a few lines. I shall continue to give you news of myself from time to time, until I can eventually greet you in your own home in the *North*. Yes, one day I think I shall come & stay put up there. Give my best wishes to your dear wife, & remember

Your friend
Fritz Delius

DELIUS TO EDVARD GRIEG

Chalet des Lilas
a la Chaumiere
Ville d'Avray
(Seine & Oise)
(31 December 1888)

My dear Grieg,

Just a few words to say "Happy New Year" to you and your wife and to wish and hope that you will enjoy very good health through the coming year, both of you. How time passes! a whole year has gone by since we were together at my place on the 4th floor in Harkortstrasse and drank Benedictine punch and the ringing of bells filled the room when we all clinked glasses, and we shall, I know, be together at many more New Years. Let's see now whether I am not right. I might almost go so far as to say that I would eat "Beckling"* with plea- sure if only I were up there in the North with you now. It is not impossible that I shall meet you in London "Beginning of February", didn't you say? and not impossible too that you may get to hear my symphonic poem "Hiawatha". I have written to Herr Manns about it, and I should very much like you to hear it. I am about to start on something about which I shall write rather later. In the meantime accept my very best wishes and give my kindest regards to Frau Grieg.

Yours
Fritz Delius

*Bokling is a type of smoked herring, whose strong taste was not enjoyed by Delius.

DELIUS TO PERCY GRAINGER

Grez sur Loing
Seine & Marne
10th June 1907

Dear Grainger!

I just received your card and am very glad you like "Appalachia".* In a week or so I shall send you "Paris" which is shortly going to be published & which will have to be arranged for piano. I have proposed you to my Editors & if the work interests you, perhaps you might undertake it. I believe they pay fairly well. Otto Singer did "Appalachia". Professor Buths of Dusseldorf arranged Paris for 2 pianos – I will also send you his arrangement with my full score.

Perhaps when I come to England you will be able to let me have the score of Green Bushes which I should just love to have. In the summer I have always a great longing to go to Norway & live among the Mountains. I love the light nights so. Which way will you go? Let me know also when. The feeling of nature I think is what I like so much in Grieg's best things You have it too & I think we all 3 have something in common. I wont swear that I shan't turn up on the steamer when you go to Bergen. If Grieg were only young & well enough to go into the hills we might have a lovely time. Give my kindest regards to your mother & believe me

ever your friend
Frederick Delius

I wish you a tremendous success for your concert & shall think of you on the 15th.

DELIUS TO PERCY GRAINGER

April 29, 1914

What pleasure your letter gave me, dear friend! You are always the one who sends me good news from England – I love your impulsive letters – they are so entirely yourself and just like your music which you know I love so much. I feel we have an enormous lot in common and that you understand better than anyone what I am trying to do – I was so happy to hear of your success in Torquay. Do you know that in Bradford they are giving a whole concert of my

---

*Grainger had written from London on 8 June: 'A thousand thanks for the Appalachia score. How interesting it is. Of course I shall just love to show it to Grieg & I bear him your messages'.

work. I proposed you should play the Concerto – it is on November 27th and I do hope you are not engaged....Can't you come over here and pay me a visit with your Mother. The spring has been simply divine – The garden is full of lilacs and Laburnums in full bloom – Try and come – I have 2 new orchestra pieces – In June we come to London for a fortnight – you must either come before or come back with me – you will love it here – it is out of this world –

Ever so much love to you and your mother.

Your loving friend
Frederick Delius.

What pleasure your letter gave me, dear friend.

In the following letter Delius shows many of the frustrations, which present day artists share, about the inability of the English to show enthusiasm and to take risks. From this letter we get a picture of the prodigious output of the composer.

DELIUS TO PERCY GRAINGER

44 Belsize Park Gardens NW.3
16th January 1919

Your letter, dear old pal, arrived here like a flash of sunshine & I cannot tell you what pleasure it gave me. I was delighted to hear that 'Life's Dance' was so well performed by Stransky & his Orchestra & also so well received. Wood gave the first performance of my new Orchestral Ballad – Eventyr (Once upon a time) after Asbjornsen – He gave a ripping good performance & took no end of trouble with it – I have a wild shout in it (20 men behind) which came off very well. I shall bring all my new works to America when I come – Your letter encouraged me very much to come out next season 1919-20 – Say in October or November. My new manuscript works are –

1) Requiem (in memory of all young artist fallen in the war. – *Not religious)* for Baritone & Soprano solo, Mixed Chorus & Orchestra
2) Concerto for Violin, Violoncello & Orchestra
3) Violin Concerto
4) Eventyr (once upon a time) (after Asbjornsen)
5) Sonata for Violoncello

6) Dance Rhapsody No 2.

7) Poem of Life & Love Orchestra
   all manuscript

Then there are several works published, but awaiting a first performance –

1) Song of the High Hills Orchestra & chorus (small)
   published by F.E.C. Leuckart, Leipzig

2) an Arabesk (J.P. Jacobsen) Baritone Solo, Chorus & Orchestra
   published by the Universal Edition Vienna –

It would be splendid if some of these works could be produced whilst I am in America. Your energy & enthusiasm is so wonderful & such a contrast to these dull countrymen of mine Oh! how dull & unresponsive this country is – I am just longing for a bit of American alertness and vivacity – I also want to visit California & have a look at the Pacific Ocean. We are both just longing for a change of climate & scenery & surroundings –

I forgot 1 new work – quite short –

8) Song before Sunrise for small orchestra

& my Violin Sonata has not been played in America – & then there are 4 Elizabethan Songs: published by Winthrop Rogers & 2 a capella Chorus's

To be sung a summer night on the water –

My wife is writing to your Mother & telling her all the news – I am looking forward hugely to being in America with you What a time we shall have – I'll conduct the Concerto & you play it – Hurrah!!

Ever your loving friend
Frederick Delius

The following letter was written by Jelka, Delius' wife, to Grainger's mother, in which she passed on all the news of the Delius' travails during the War and of Frederick's music, but also included all the gossip of musical London.

44, Belsize Park Gardens
London N.W.3
14.1.1919

Dearest Mrs Grainger,

We were both perfectly delighted with your letter from Dec 13th received this morning – It was such *good* news that 'Life's Dance' was performed with such success. How I should have loved to applaud with Percy and you – I once sat next to him at a Delius-performance and it was so splendid to see him love it so!! The people here are always *so heavy*! We came to London [at the] beginning of Sept. and were thoroughly tired of our 3 years exile in France, entirely away from music. Since the big German push last spring poor little Grez has been in the War-Zone and life became intolerable and anyhow Grez was all *but* invaded by the enemy and without the Americans there was really no hope left. Fred had been writing such beautiful music during the quiet years of war – quiet at least in Grez – So we took all the manuscripts, our beautiful Gaugin pictures and left our home once more – perfectly sick at heart – We went right down to Biarritz where we soon got the good news of the turning tide – none too soon! America had done *wonderfully* reconstructing all France nobody here in England appreciates it enough. But we who have lived in France know it and shall never forget it. Also our eyes are turned to Wilson now. Our house in Grez was commandeered by the French military – and has been full of officers, and an officers mess part of the time and is still full of them. We only came back to lock away and save what could be saved and left the house to them and came here. Fred was thirsting for music. We are living in a furnished flat up in Hampstead and by special permission brought a little French maid along – I crossed the sea wearing a swimming tricot and the manuscripts I had tied up in watertight bags and would have swum with them fixed on to a life-belt! But, almost: alas! nothing happened after all these preparations.

Things here looked rather dull when we came – Only dear old Wood was valiantly doing his Prom's. But Beecham has entirely thrown up Concert-conducting – He only cares for his opera-schemes – and there even he is more

Impresario than conductor. He has Pitt young Goossens and Harrison as conductors. As they give all the dull old operas it is really not very interesting. He is also not conducting the Philharmonic any more – He was too erratic and the Public became less and less. Now Norman O'Neill has made a great effort to reconstruct the Phil. Balfour Gardiner has helped financially and they have Geoffrey Toye Landon Ronald and Boult as conductors. Boult is to conduct Fred's new Violin Concerto there on the 30th Jan – Sammons playing it. They have put in an extra rehearsal, as Fred otherwise would have not allowed it to be performed – He cannot bear the way they have here of preparing so insufficiently. A few days ago Wood gave a new Orchestral Work of Freds 'Eventyr' (once upon a time) It is based on the Norwegian folk tales of Ahbjornson. It is a charming, most beautiful work and Wood took enormous trouble over it and did it really awfully well. Of course all *could not* perhaps be quite realized in this first performance, but it was a spirited performance and the music is quite adorable – so Norwegian – the little trolls cantering along on the "Vidder's", the Huldre, the Peasant's – The spirit of the whole thing was there out in that beloved nature. I think he has realized all that so well in the very longing of his heart to go to Norway – impossible on account of the War. There was an enormous audience and the piece was awfully well received –I felt as if I was at last throwing off the war – breathing the Queen's Hall rehearsal – atmosfere – then the public, the enthusiasm and all quite thrilled me.

Fred has also written a beautiful Violin-Cello Sonata. It is all of a swing, lovely. Beatrice Harrison has already played it twice at her 2 recitals. Winthrop-Rogers is editing it. I think it will be a great success when Beatr. Harr. takes it over to America. The Harrisons are also studying Fred's Double Concerto Violin and Cello – and it will probably be played in March. Hamilton Harty conducts quite often now. He did the 2 short pieces (Cuckoo and Summernight) rather well. Fred would like and probably will found a new Concert-Society – appealing to a more democratic public, as they certainly seem to appreciate music more than the Society people; they are deadly.

Balfour G. is still in Wales, guarding a Prisoner's camp; I hope, tho' he won't be very long now. They are woodcutters and he does not dislike the work – walking far thro' the woods to look after them. He came to see us here and was awfully nice – so sincere and real – Cyril Scott we met once at Lady Cunards he looked rather tired, but seemed quite alright. The O'Neills are bringing up their new baby. Austin is in the Beecham Opera, Bax has inherited no end of money from his father and Geoffrey Toye also lots from a brother officer.

16.1.19

Dear Mrs Grainger – will you ever find time to read all this? Since I began this letter Percy's splendid letter arrived and we just loved it. It was so awfully nice of him to collect all the cuttings and send them, it gives us such a good idea of it all – We hope most fervently that Percy will *soon* be given back to you and to his glorious artistic career. How lucky they did not send him over here. It has been too dreadful – Fred's nephew, only 19 and an only son was killed just before the end.

We are *awfully keen* about going to America. If it were only possible to earn a little money, either by conducting or editions of Fred's works – as the cost of everything over there is so formidable. For instance I am sure Fred could conduct his piano Concerto *very well* – Financially we have had a very trying time, as most of our money is in a German Bank – on account of editors etc – and altho' lots of it is in N. Am. Railways and South America – we cannot get it, as it is in the name of the Bank. So we must hope for a speedy conclusion of peace and then see how we stand – It has been a great worry and I hope it will soon be over. Isn't it glorious that Fred has composed such lots of lovely things during the war?

If we could we should like it best to have a *little* furnished flat or rooms in N.Y. where we could cook simple food like you seem to do. Good healthy food is so essential for Fred. I must stop now dear friends, let us hear again soon!

Most affectionately yours
JELKA DELIUS

ERIK SATIE
1866–1925

Erik Satie was born in Honfleur in Normandy. Both his parents were composers and at the age of seventeen he spent a year at the Paris Conservatoire. He was greatly influenced by Wagner but at the same time Satie was very much his own man. His whimsy and interest and flirtation with Surrealism and Dada-ism often stood in the way of recognition. He used to write his scores in red ink without bar lines, often making witty illustrations and giving his compositions punning titles.

ERIK SATIE TO SUZANNE VALADON

Paris, the 11th of the month of March 93

Dear little Biqui,
Impossible
to stop thinking about your whole
being; you are in Me complete; everywhere,
I see nothing but your exquisite
eyes, your gentle hands
and your little child's feet.
You, you are happy; My poor thoughts
are not going to wrinkle your transparent forehead;
any more than worry at not seeing Me.
For Me there is only the icy
solitude that creates an emptiness in my head
and fills my heart with sorrow.
Don't forget that your poor friend
hopes to see you at least at one of these three rendezvous:

In the early part of the 20th century Satie enjoyed a 'clubby' existence, mixing with the intellectuals in Paris. These included Apollinaire the poet, Francis Poulenc and Darius Milhaud. They were to perform at the Vieux Colombier and Satie called the group the 'Nouveaux Jeunes'.
Satie corresponded with Poulenc even before meeting him. In 1915, when he was fifteen and still attending the Conservatoire, Poulenc had the idea of conducting a survey into what some of the 'well-known'

musicians of the day thought about Cesar Franck. Debussy, for example, was critical, saying that he didn't write in the cultural tradition of their own country. Satie's opinion was different.

ERIK SATIE TO FRANCIS POULENC

October 1915

Monsieur,

Everything leads me to suppose that Franck was a huge musician. His work is astonishingly Franckist, in the best sense of the word.

A great Paris publisher claims that Franck was lazy.

– Oui, Monsieur.

If that is true, Franck was very blameworthy, since laziness is a very nasty thing, not to be recommended, especially in a worker.

This opinion is entirely personal and in no way binding.

Please accept, Sir, the amiable amiabilities of him who is

Erik Satie

P.S. I am not 'well-known': I am a 'young quinquagenarian'.

Satie became very involved with the Paris Dadaists and particularly with Francis Picabia with whom he indulged in vaguely pornographic jokes. He later collaborated with him in *Relache*, which he was to describe as a 'ballet obscene'.

ERIK SATIE TO FRANCIS PICABIA

Arcueil-Cachan,
3 January 1921

Cher Ami – all my cordial good wishes – Cordial-Medoc.

I have one *pensée* for your magazine: 'I would like to play around a really bulging piano'.

Erik Satie

P.S. That seems to me very proper and very artistic without seeming to be. Bien à vous.

Erik Satie

Arcueil-Cachan,
30 Jan. 1921

Mon cher Ami – Did you receive a little *pensée*: 'I would like to play around a really bulging piano'?

Here's another, just as neat: 'It isn't good manners to talk about the cock-up of a question...

I'd be very pleased if you liked these two 'things' enough to print them in your estimable periodical.

It's vanity, I know; so I beg you to forgive me for this wish.

Amicalement votre:

Erik Satie

Satie's two 'pensées' appeared in the Pilhaou-Thibaou long before the publication of the Surrealist Manifesto and later were to be included in the anthologies of Dada and Surrealist theatre.

In 1922 he wrote an article on Stravinsky for Vanity Fair. His approach was extraordinary as is seen by the following letter to Stravinsky, asking for information.

ERIK SATIE TO IGOR STRAVINSKY

Arcueil-Cachan
3 July 1922

Mon Cher Stravinsky –

Bonjour, Cher Ami. How are you?

...I have a great service to ask of you. It is this: A big American magazine has asked me to write an article on you. I hope you don't see any objections to that. This article has to be *'light and easy'* for the reader, while remaining fundamentally serious.

Would you be so kind as to send me;

– name and forename;

–birthplace;

–date of birth;

–your teachers (in order);

–a chronological list of your works (dates, where performed, publishers).

Indicate the main pamphlets, the most important articles written about you.

I am relying completely on you and ask you to please suggest what you *particularly* want me to say about you.

Send me all this as soon as possible, Cher Ami, I beg and implore you.

Amicalement votre:

Erik Satie

Arcueil-Cachan,
9 August 1922

Mon Cher et Illustre Ami – It was kind of you to write me such a friendly no-note.

I haven't forgotten you because I'm working on the article about you every day.

I do not allow myself to judge you, not being a 'schoolmaster' like those I don't want to talk about: they are too stupid, poor fools. That's not surprising: on top of that they're idiots.

No, cher Ami, I do not pass judgement on you: I admire you and only talk about you as the great 'luminary' that you are. It would be impossible for me to confuse you with the 'wretched plodders' whom you know as well as I do. What miserable 'clods'! Yes.

I'll send you *Parade*.

Will you please convey my regards to Madame Stravinsky, Cher Ami.

Bien a vous, je suis

ES

Stravinsky said that he took to Satie at their very first meeting. 'He's a sly one. He was full of guile and intelligently malicious.'

RALPH VAUGHAN WILLIAMS
1872–1958

Vaughan Williams was born in Gloucestershire and was educated at Cambridge and the Royal College of Music. From his early twenties he became interested in the collection and study of English folk-songs and throughout his life he remained involved with popular traditions in music such as the Folk Dance movement. He also edited the English Hymnal.

He wrote much orchestral music, including nine symphonies and other orchestral works, including the *Fantasia on a Theme of Thomas Tallis*. His songs and arrangement of English Folk songs became popular favourites and were quickly adopted by school-choirs and amateur music makers.

RALPH VAUGHAN WILLIAMS TO THE MORNING POST

Sep 24 1904
10 Barton Street
Westminster

Sir

Your correspondent, Mr Stewart Gowe, is of the opinion that there are no folk-songs left in Essex. Last Spring I spent a fortnight in an Essex village only twenty miles from London, and there and in the neighbourhood I noted down over fifty genuine folk-songs. Most of the songs had beautiful and interesting tunes. As to the words, some were old ballads such as "Robin Hood and Pedlar" or "The Green Glove", some came off the ballad sheets, as for instance "The Lost Lady" and others were regular country songs such as "The Painful Plough". Has Mr Gowe carefully explored his own district and made sure that the traditional songs have died out?

Yours etc.

R. Vaughan Williams

The following letter is the first of two communications which have survived from Vaughan Williams to Delius, both dated 1907.

146

13 Cheyne Walk S.W.

Dear Mr Delius

I hope you will not think I am making a very audacious request – I should so much like to show you some of my work. I have had it in my mind (and especially now that I have heard your beautiful concerto) that I should profit very much by your advice and if you saw my work you might be able to suggest ways in which I cd improve myself – either by going to Paris or not. Have you ever any time to spare – and if you have would you allow me to come and see you.

I don't know if I ought to ask this on so slight an acquaintance.

Yours very truly

R. Vaughan Williams

Oct 24th (1907)

Moeran's choral setting of words from Robert Nichol's play *Don Juan Tenorio the Great* was written in 1934 for the Norwich Philharmonic Society and is inscribed 'To the Memory of Frederick Delius', who had died on 10 June 1934.

The White Gates

Westcott Road

Dorking

February 8 (1935)

Dear Moeran

Many thanks for the copy of the Nocturne – I thought it beautiful – I think the references to Delius in the Press are absurd. Doubtless if Delius had not existed it might not have been written. Just as Delius would not have been written without Grieg or Grieg without Schumann and so on back to Tubal Cain.

I find in your work a distinction of style that I fail to find usually in Delius with the notable exception of the Wedding Procession (*not* the Paradise Garden in Romeo and Juliet.)

Yrs

R Vaughan Williams

As with the First World War the Second World War had far-reaching effects on the music-making and composers of the world. Once again in Great Britain the problem of whether to play compositions by German composers had to be faced.

ADRIAN BOULT TO RALPH VAUGHAN WILLIAMS

October 26th 1939

Private

Thanks for the second letter, I return your B.B.C. reply. I did not write sooner because I have been moving about and wanted to think over your letter a little more carefully.

I think you will realize that in a post mortem of this period I do not intend to be unvocal, and I think you will guess how I feel about the whole matter. I have perhaps been too easy-going in the past and only occasionally put forward the plea that I am the only broadcasting Director of Music in any broadcasting organisation who is not absolute master of his own programme policy. Between these four walls I do not think resignation would be any use or threats of that kind because I have reason to believe, though I have not been officially told, that a certain amount of the instructions that came to us in regard to these emergency programmes both at the present time and when they were planned some time before the crisis, had emanated from Whitehall, and I do not think Whitehall, or that part of it that is capable of giving instructions that the public are to be amused at all cost even when they have just been told that a battleship has been sunk, cares whether A.B.C. or X.Y.Z. is Director of Music of the B.B.C.

I do not want to make any excuses, but it is a fact that between September 2nd and 11th nine symphonies were performed by the following composers, Haydn, Beethoven, Dvorak, Mendelssohn, Mozart, Schubert, i.e. one a day. Did you realise this? I admit that many of them were at impossible times to listen, but, rightly or wrongly, we have assumed (no doubt here again under instructions) that most of Britain had gone on to a shift system and would be listening at all times of the day. Did you see that delightful letter from Manchester in last week's Radio Times about the eight o'clock Concerts? It made me want to do one every day.

In regard to the enclosure, which I return, I have taken steps to see that the Director-General personally sees your letter. He has been travelling a good deal, and it may have been passed on in his absence.

Walford Davies was a composer and professor of counterpoint at the Royal College of Music, Conductor of the London Bach Choir and Master of the King's Musick.

The Deanery
Bristol
9th November, 1939

Dear Ralph,

The various efforts to promote music-making through every part of the country are clarifying, and Adrian, Thatcher and I met Barnes of the B.B.C. yesterday and got approval for instituting a weekly broadcast to give, by word of mouth and by examples sung and/or played there and then, all possible practical help to amateur music-making.

The scheme is meant, and will be conceived throughout, as an attempted national service to music-makers everywhere and not as a broadcast 'turn', more or less entertaining to listeners generally.

It will be necessary to ask those who have done things to come and suggest to listening amateurs how things are done. And I am afraid you are the first we are obliged to trouble about it.

We have been offered to begin with an introductory set of six talks at a *Sunday* time when everybody is likely to be listening, 8.45 to 9.0 pm, just before the 9 o'clock News. I am to introduce these on November 26th, and on the four succeeding dates – December 3rd, 10th, 24th – four orders of music-making in all districts throughout the black-out of winter are to be dealt with. I promised Adrian I would write and beg you to take the first of these on December 3rd. I was afraid it would mean going to London to do that Sunday evening, unless indeed you felt able and inclined to come on the Saturday to Bristol and do it from here with Adrian to arrange any illustrating of your points (solo or ensemble) which would be much better.

Yours
HWD

GUSTAV HOLST
1874–1934

Holst was born at Cheltenham (another Gloucestershire composer) and started composing from a very young age. He began his professiona. life as the village organist and conductor of village choral societies and at nineteen went to the Royal College of Music where he spent five years. He was taught composition by Stanford. To earn his living he played as a trombonist in the Scottish Symphony Orchestra. From 1906 he was the Director of Music at St Paul's Girls' School. At about the same time he became connected with Morley College, where he developed many musical activities. As well as giving us *The Planets Suite* and *The Hymn of Jesus*, one of his finest gifts was communicating his love of music.

During the First World War he was asked to go to Salonica to organize musical activities among the soldiers. He was very successful in this and sent home for large quantities of songbooks, textbooks and copies of Byrd's three-part Mass.

HOLST TO EDWIN EVANS

St Pauls Girls School, W6
Sep 22 (1918)

Dear Evans

My 'Planet' pieces are to be done at Queen's Hall next Sunday morning Sep.29 10.30 to 1.30. From 12.15 to 1.30 will be the best time. Boult is conducting. It will be a purely private affair but please tell anyone who you think would care to come. Entrance North door.

I am going to Salonica for the YMCA and in order to be more help to them I am dropping my 'von'.

Yr faithfully
G.T. Holst

HOLST TO HIS PUPILS AT MORLEY COLLEGE

8.30 pm. January 25th, 1919
In a tent near the ruins of a shelled city on the borders of Bulgaria

Dear Friends, I have just been lecturing and playing to some soldiers for an hour and a half, and am now sitting in my tent wondering how the concert is going on and trying to imagine the sound of your voices and instruments. In time I hope I shall get heaps of letters from you letting me know how it all goes, and whether Dr. Terry is pleased with you.

On the whole I am having a very good time. But the army is scattered over an enormous area, and even when you reach a place very often you find the camp breaking up and very few men left. Of course one is very glad that things like that are happening, but it is sometimes a little disconcerting. I am nearly a hundred miles north of Salonica, and have come all the way by motor car along with a sleeping bag, two blankets, lots to eat and drink, and about a dozen parcels of music. I had to cross the Struma valley, where so much fighting took place. Also I have had a long walk through the ruined city out on to the hills beyond, jumping over trenches, avoiding – or not avoiding – barbed wire, exploring dug-outs and gun emplacements, finally visiting an ancient Acropolis, the ruins of which were cleverly used by the Bulgars in a manner which was as horrible as it was clever. But the greatest sight I saw was also the greatest sight I have ever seen; indeed, I felt I was witnessing the greatest scene on earth: I saw Greek peasants and their oxen ploughing the battlefield for the first time since the fighting ceased!

Good luck to them and to you.

Yours sincerely
G T Holst

P.S. – Jan. 27th. I returned to Salonica last night, and have been out all day motoring in a 'tin Lizzie' with the Pardar wind blowing – a really cold job. After making arrangements to form a choir in one camp, ditto plus a harmony class in a second, settling final arrangements for a lecture at a third, discussing the possibility of forming a sing-song during a cinema show by throwing the words of a song on the screen (owing to the non-arrival of song books) at a fourth, and finally conducting the Unfinished Symphony and the Mendelssohn violin concerto with the splendid Artillery School orchestra founded by Captain Colles, the musical critic of the *Times*, who is now in England. The orchestra was led by a Morleyite – Gunner Keyes, who sends his greeting to you all.

FRANK BRIDGE
1879–1941

Frank Bridge was one of a long tradition of distinguished composers who were also teachers. He was a pupil of Stanford at the Royal College of Music and in turn taught Benjamin Britten composition there. He wrote many oratorios, cantatas, anthems and textbooks.

FRANK BRIDGE TO BENJAMIN BRITTEN

Friston Field
May 3 1937

My dear Benjy,

I intended sending you a line before this. It is an odd thing that music has to have really the right approach in order to make its own mark. I felt rather a lot of sympathy for you about Friday night's performance. Beyond 'Our Hunting Fathers' I heard almost no other words and this left everyone wondering precisely what it was all about. Even Marg. 'Over the air' didn't hear the words. But, both Ethel and I got much more of your work at Norwich with all its shortcomings and bad conditions of rehearsal etc. The quintessence of disappointment on your face was so marked that had I had a few minutes alone with you, I might have consoled you with the fact that many a good work has begun its public life much in the same indifferent way. It is extremely hard to bear, but one *must* and I suppose *does* anyway. Of course, a real blot on the programme having a further display of xylophone colour immediately, was perfectly sickening for us, and surely for you too?

You'll have to reconcile yourself about even the smaller public getting to know your work. Opportunities are not likely to be many. When we get together again remind me of this, there are a few things I should like to say sometime.

In the meantime try to get on with something important and forget the temporary nuisances of a composer. On occasions like Friday, it is a mistake not to be ready to put in an appearance. Even if audiences don't enthuse after a performance, they *may* like the *composer* when he appears.

But do cheer up,
love from us both,

Ever,
FB

P.S. Show me what the press did say. I noticed and thought a section of the Observer's notice had been cut out by the editor for want of space. If it were so then such manners are deplorable.

Friston Field
[undated]

My dear Benjamin (as Sophie Wyss would have it)

You never pointed out to me that Benjamin was the signature of the tribe! I imagine you have had your permit to stay in the USA seen to long ago, unless you are buzzing back to Canada. Ralph said he would invite me to hear a run through of the Concerto by Paul and Henry Boys, but it never came off, although I was in London on the very day that it did happen, by chance. That's all I know about it. There are rumours of a Piano Quartet with Orchestra for Toronto and a Revue for New York. I wish I felt happier about this last (with the New Statesman writing of the two recruiting sergeants....being away in America).

As you probably know, there was a complete breakdown of programmes and entertainments generally on the B.B.C. when hostilities began. Quite apart from the removal to 'somewhere in England', no one seems to know precisely what upset the organisation. But upset or upside down it assuredly was. Everything was cancelled. For the first five or six weeks, except for news, it was quite difficult to understand what was being aimed at! However, there is recently some improvement. They managed to get Gracie Fields to broadcast sometime before she entertained the troops in France. And Sir A.B. 'did' the *Eroica* just before midnight, and people give piano recitals at 7.10 am and so the art of giving the crowd what they want is now thoroughly understood.

You can say nothing appreciative about America and the Americans that is not endorsed by me. That is, all those that I know are a part of one's own small world. They add to it rather an important section. One where queries and question marks are taboo, a kind of buffer between inevitable old age and the last remnant of youth and any other fantastic expression which includes rest, sympathy and personal interest. In other terms, I never knew how much I had been without until I found myself in possession of it, and since 1923 too!

Upon looking closely at your address, I see it is not Coney Island Home. No connection with our own Colney Hatch. Oh dear, dear no!! I never could make out that American enthusiasm for Ville. I always thought they felt it rather 'chic'...a touch of French, say. Now – Amitystadt – what about it?

Some years ago, driving on Long Island, I remember getting out of the car, the road having ceased abruptly on a sandy shore, bending down and swishing my hands in the sea sending a few ripples straight over to Cornwall. Just a sentimental moment, of course.

We have had some of the most fiendishly bad weather ever in our Friston history.

At long last, the billeting officer foisted two evacuated children upon us, they are Croydon kids.

All this is a nasty socialist move – make the blighters that have six inches more cubic space than they need, than they positively need etc. All very well, then, but to force one to look after evacuees is the limit. One's personal attention is demanded, and enforced. Think of it! To be caught, because one has a cottage, to take kids, see that they have baths, cure their colds – poor Bill – and me, and her not able to leave Friston because of ... Defence of the Realm Regulations.

And you've no idea what you miss...! All good wishes for Xmas, my dear Benjie.

Understand this if you can, Tosc. [anini] gave one in London with NY orch, a super performance of *Eroica* of which you have heard before now. But Bill and I heard a really poor show of Tsch. *Romeo and Juliet* in NY only last year, and other things too. But, dear Benjie, – hold tight – only those capable of criticism understand the truth of criticism, very few, I fear, do not attribute base or false motives to serious criticism, in fact – as you and I know – the entire world of music is out of step...with our Johnny! Isn't that so?

JOHN IRELAND
1879–1962

John Ireland's parents were well-known authors and he was brought up in a literary atmosphere, meeting many men and women of letters. He too studied composition under Stanford at the Royal College of Music. He is most known for his songs which include his setting of Masefield's *Sea Fever*. His works for piano are delicate and sensitive.

JOHN IRELAND TO A FRIEND

1954

I have listened twice to Britten's new opera *The Turn of the Screw*. I am no judge of opera as such, but this contains the most remarkable and original music I have ever heard from the pen of a British composer – and it is on a firmly *diatonic* and *tonal* basis. Also, what he has accomplished in sound by the use of only 13 instruments was, to me, inexplicable; almost miraculous. This is not to say I *liked* the music, but it is gripping, vital and often terrifying. I am now (perhaps *reluctantly*) compelled to regard Britten as possessing ten times the musical talent, intuition and ability of all other living British composers put together.

PERCY GRAINGER
1882–1961

Grainger was born in Melbourne, Australia and died in White Plains, New York. From the age of fourteen he lived mostly in the United States. He trained as pianist in Frankfurt with Busoni and he first appeared in London at the age of eighteen.

In April 1907 he met Delius who was to exert a strong musical and personal influence on his life. Delius often asked Grainger to go and stay with him but as a result of the First World War this was to prove impossible until 1919. About this time Thomas Beecham had begun to include Delius's works in his programmes and whenever possible Grainger went to hear them. The two composers corresponded regularly and Delius valued Grainger's letters enormously. It is almost certain that Beecham's interest in Grainger's music came about through Delius' recommendation.

Svinklov. Jutland
9.9.07

Delius

Warmest thanks for your kind sympathetic card. Isn't it too sad, darling sweet little Grieg's death? I had such an unspeakably happy & uplifting time with them. I left them about a month ago.

He was always talking of you, affectionately & admiringly, & told me lots of jolly anecdotes of your trips together in the High Hills.

I showed him Appalachia & played him bits & he studied often in the score, & was *keenly interested.*

On the very day I got Mrs Grieg's wire telling me of his death I was planning to write you & convey to you Grieg's delight when I proposed to him that I'd ask you to send him a score of Appalachia.

3 Cheers re your Brigg Fair work.

Longing to see it & you.

In frantic haste, & warm thanks for your friendly sympathy

Yrs ever
Percy Grainger

c/o E.L Robinson – 7 Wigmore St. Lond. W.

Am playing at the 1st Grieg Memorial concert in Denmark Friday next

In 1909 Percy Grainger and a troupe of artists sailed for New Zealand, where he toured the main cities of both islands. Grainger, like Grieg and Vaughan Williams, was very interested in folk music and in particular, Maori music. Whenever possible, with the help of two Maori guides, Maggie and Pomeri, he went to listen to it and note it down. In Otaki he discovered Knocks and his music, which he vividly describes in a letter to Roger Quilter, the composer and a fellow enthusiast of folk music

PERCY GRAINGER TO ROGER QUILTER

I met a dear old man...born here, son of a settler, I should say, brought up in the country when Maoris swarmed and whites were scarce; $\frac{1}{2}$ (at least) native in feeling, married to a Maori, very chummily pally with his handsome but erratic $\frac{1}{2}$ breed sons, quite a card he is. Kind and easygoing to animals; they browse in his unkempt garden, doesn't kill flies if he can help it and takes phonograph records of every bit of native music he can. 2 years ago Raratongan natives were brought over to Christchurch Exhibition. They sang gloriously. This old man phonographed them. Nobody else did seemingly. His name is Knocks...I came to hear his Maori records, but he made me hear the Raratongan records and I straightway noted them down in his cob-house from afternoon early to 5 the next morn. The old man stayed up to 2 o'clock with me, and he and $\frac{1}{2}$ breeds and I had great fun manning the phonograph and chatting and getting on well together and feeding on tea and bread and butter. That old chap is a dear trustful tolerant (though a bit bitter against the whites) kindlesouled born artist nature; you don't find that sort in Australia.

These Raratongan things are the strongest impressions I've met since the Faero dance tunes. These are dance music also. But *polyphonic*. They have *real harmony*, and of course tons of rhythmic delights. Sometimes their spirit is very sweet, rocking and kittenish, and at times fierce and rending like tiger claws, but always it is great larks...Red flowers in shining blueblack hair, the easy graceful gait of dance instincts of folk shortly ago fighters and maneaters; there is lots of fun ahead. I am taking some phonograph records of maori songs myself. *Not* sung in harmony ever as far as I can make out; but queer interesting intervals they use, and they sing and recite like heroes; such wantonness, laziness, energy, unselfbeknownst attack, and strong coaxing throbbing voices...

Percy Grainger became passionate about the music of Knocks. The cylinders of their music whilst they were with Grainger are now preserved in Melbourne and are amongst the few authentic recordings of the polyphonic singing from Raratonga.

His tour in the Antipodes made him an even more eccentric-looking figure. The influence of the Maoris had made him very fond of bright colours and he persuaded his mother to make him shirts and shorts out of brilliantly hued towelling which he found comfortable both to teach and to go running in.

IGOR STRAVINSKY
1882–1971

He was born near St Petersburg and died in New York. Stravinsky initially trained in the law but after meeting Rimsky-Korsakov whilst travelling in Germany, he decided to devote himself to music. In his mid-twenties he met the impresario of the Russian Ballet, Serge Diaghilev and after this, Paris became his musical home. He wrote a series of successful ballet scores but he didn't really cause much controversy until he wrote *The Rite of Spring* which largely ignored existing conventions of harmony, rhythm and form.

Whilst living in Paris he bcame a great friend of Francis Poulenc.

IGOR STRAVINSKY TO FRANCIS POULENC

1 January 1923

Happy New Year, my dear Poulenc.

I did not see very much of you at the concert. Your hasty departure afterwards and your rather despondent mood during the concert – what was it all about? Or am I being indiscreet?

As for me, I left the concert in utter disgust and despair. So did Ansermet. Actually, the rehearsal had promised quite a good performance of *Mavra*. And then you saw what the singers did to me. Apart from how my music is performed, there is a great deal to be said about where it is performed. Most places tend to be designed for dressed-up music, whereas mine – the kind I have been writing for the past two years – is naked. And then it finds itself in the hands of couturiers, against whom brave Ansermet struggles desperately. I am in a very bad mood, and with good reason.

Your Stravinsky

He became friends with Prokofiev, although Prokofiev was apt to be jealous of Stravinsky. At one stage they were both working for Diaghilev.

One example of the tension in the relationship of the two composers is shown here, documented by Vera Stravinsky and Robert Craft.

'After a concert in Warsaw, Stravinsky had traced his hand in a woman's autograph album, in his case a not infrequent form of responding to a request for a 'souvenir'...Later, when Prokofiev was asked to sign the same book, he inscribed a mocking remark under the drawing. Stravinsky read about this in a Paris newspaper and wrote to Prokofiev.'

STRAVINSKY TO PROKOFIEV

20 December 1933

Dear Seriozha,

I send this clipping which appeared recently in the Paris newspapers. I suppose that your interpretation of your joke in the album of the Warsaw woman had another character than the one given to it by these unknown-to-me slanderers in the newspapers. Surely it cannot have been your intention to laugh at me as a pianist – or even as a conductor. My hand, drawn in the album, both plays and conducts, and not so shamefully, I think, that people might make stupid and nasty fun of me. No doubt many people object to my activity as a performer, but it is the only way to avoid the grimaces of other interpreters of my music. Devotedly and with love, Igor Stravinsky.

Prokofiev answered on 21 December

I much appreciate your indulgence for this affair in the newspapers. It has afflicted me terribly. Now it is time to forget that whole period – when you spoke badly about my music as well as about what I wrote in the woman's album.

IGOR STRAVINSKY TO FRANCIS POULENC

Nice,
6 April 1931

Mon cher Poulenc, very touched by your note and the article on my *Symphony of Psalms*. I could not have wished for a better Easter present. You are truly good, and that is what I always find again and again in your music. May God protect you.

I may be in Paris at the end of May. If so, I will certainly come to your concert.

Your Igor

SERGE PROKOFIEV
1891–1953

Prokofiev was born in Sontsovka, in Russia, and died on the same day as Josef Stalin in Moscow at the age of sixty-one.

The following letters were written whilst he was a pupil at the St Petersburg Conservatory during the rumblings of the Russian Revolution in 1905. He became widely known as a virtuoso pianist and Rimsky-Korsakov was one of his teachers. At this time he appeared not to be concerned about the impending revolution, or, at least, only in so far as it might affect his studies. However, in 1948, along with other leading musicians, he came under censure by the Soviet authorities for the alleged 'formalistic distortions and anti-democratic tendencies of his music'.

He writes, ' We reached Petersburg exactly three days after the people, led by Gapon, had come to the square in front of the Winter Palace with a petition to the Tsar and had been fired on. The city was now externally quiet but seemed to be quaking from underground explosions, just as the ripples from a stone thrown into a pond continue to spread for a long time afterward'.

PROKOFIEV TO HIS FATHER

Petersburg,
February 5 1905

Just imagine! They started a strike at the Conservatory. Today when I went for my harmony lesson I saw that little knots of people had gathered everywhere, students of sixteen and seventeen, shouting and making a lot of noise. The class met anyway, but not even half of the students were there. One of them, Kankarovich, didn't come until after two o'clock instead of at one. He had been at a meeting in the Little Auditorium, where more than forty people had gathered. They all argued, and made a noise, and finally signed their names. The main thing was that they didn't have any aim. In general, the students are protesting, for example, against the fact that one of their number in a certain class is a soldier who shot at the workers during the disturbances, and that they do not want to have a 'murderer' as a fellow-student. Second that Auer, the professor of violin, is very irritable and is always scolding the students; that, in their opinion, he dropped one student for no reason at all; that at every lesson he spends ten minutes more with one girl student he knows than with the others. Finally, that today one of the attendants behaved rudely, saying they were nothing but 'scum', that they had killed the grand duke, etc.

My exercises were rather well done, although two unusual mistakes were found: cross-relations.

After the lesson Kankarovic began to make a speech, explaining to Lyadov why they had called a meeting. In general he talked nonsense. As Lyadov put it, these things are trivial matters that could be settled without a lot of fuss simply by going to the director. And our whole class disagreed with Kankarovich, saying that they were always protesting over trifles, and that we might suffer if the Conservatory were closed: we should lose a year, and we would lose the tuition money we had paid.

> He later remarked, "This shows the influence of the talk I heard at home, which I of course repeated. My mother's view-point was as follows: 'since we had left my father in Sontsovka and come to Petersburg so that I could study, the thing to do was study and not become involved in things we could not understand."
>
> The grand duke referred to was the uncle of Nicholas II and husband of the Czarina's sister. He was assassinated on February 4, 1905.

Petersburg,
February 13, 1905

Some people are saying that the Conservatory will be closed until September. But others are saying that it won't be closed; first, since there are many against the strike; second, because there are many adolescents there. In our class, two students – that is, one third of Lyadov's theory students – went on strike: Kankarovich and Kobylyansky. The former is one of the chief strikers and throughout his life has been a rebel. He takes part in everything – in all the meetings. Yesterday he asked me, 'What? Are you going to continue attending harmony class?' 'Of course I am,' I said. 'In that case,' he said, 'goodbye.' And turned and walked off. Just why Kobylyansky is striking, I don't know. In the first place, he is a tuition-free student. And in the second place, as a tuition-free student, he has two majors: piano and theory of composition.

Petersburg,
February 20, 1905

The concert was amazingly uninteresting: they played something long and boring by Mozart.* Berlioz's *Flight into Egypt* was also rather boring. The most interesting item was Glazunov's *Concerto for Violin and Orchestra*. The composer conducted, and Auer played the violin. The former was much applauded, but the latter was hissed for political reasons.

Petersburg,
February 23 1905

On Monday, February 21st, when I went to the Conservatory with a fugue I was taking to Winkler, I saw that the door was closed. There was a notice posted on it saying that the Conservatory would be closed on February 21, 22, and 23. There was a group of about ten students near the door. One theory student said the strikers had begun to use force, and that if anyone tried to attend classes they would evict both the students and professors from the classrooms. It was because of this that the Conservatory closed for three days. It was very distressing. We had already missed two classes with Lyadov and for Saturday before Ash Wednesday the question arose: would there be a class or not? Besides, later on Lyadov will drive us terribly hard to catch up.

Petersburg,
March 19, 1905

...During class Lyadov got a letter from the Conservatory inviting him to a meeting to consider the question of expelling those who had broken windows and had been taken to the police station.

Rimsky-Korsakov has published an interesting letter about the St. Petersburg Conservatory in a Moscow newspaper. He writes that he has already advised, several times, that the Conservatory be closed until September 1st.

---

*He later wrote: 'Then, and for a long time afterwards, I didn't like Mozart, probably because I didn't find in him those interesting harmonies and that dramatic content which especially interested me in music. My antipathy was so well defined that when someone began to praise him I would exclaim, 'How can you like Mozart!'

Lyadov says he doesn't know whether there will be any exams in music or not. It may be that they'll be held in the autumn, and maybe they'll move us up into the next class without examinations. Then next year, in the spring, when we go from counterpoint to fugue, we'll be examined in counterpoint and harmony at the same time. This isn't very likely, since we have students who could hardly pass the exam between harmony and counterpoint: Grossman, for example, and possibly Kobylyansky.

Petersburg,
March 23, 1905

Today I went to Lyadov's class. I had done seven exercises for him. He said, 'Yes today you have done the chorales much better.' And he said that twice.

I wrote to you that during the last class Lyadov received an invitation to a meeting in the Conservatory. Here is the way that session ended. Rimsky-Korsakov began to make a speech in which he condemned the actions of the board of directors. At this Bernhard, the director, who was chairman, rang the bell (to interrupt the speech), got up and left the session.

The board of directors of the Musical Society (under the chairmanship of Grand Duke Konstantin Konstantinovitch) informed Rimsky-Korsakov that he was dismissed from his position as professor because of the letter (the one I wrote to you about when you were in Moscow).

In the meantime, Bernhard has resigned. The position of director was offered to Glazunov, but he said that if Rimsky-Korsakov is dismissed from the faculty, he not only has no desire to be director of the Conservatory but will also resign from the faculty. And if Glazunov and Rimsky-Korsakov leave, they will be followed by Lyadov, Esipova, Benois, Verzhbilovich, and many others. Probably Rimsky-Korsakov will be asked to stay on.

Petersburg,
March 27, 1905

As was to be expected, after Rimsky-Korsakov was dismissed from the Conservatory, Glazunov, Lyadov, Auer, Esipova, Benois, Verzhbilovich and others resigned from the faculty.

Everyone is expressing sympathy for Rimsky-Korsakov. One hundred and thirty-one professors sent him a message of solidarity, and the Moscow musicians have protested against his dismissal. Even high school students have sent him a message of solidarity.

For next year there exists [a plan that] all students (six of us) will take group private lessons in counterpoint from Lyadov. From Lyadov and not Rimsky-Korsakov, since Rimsky-Korsakov either charges a terribly high fee for private lessons or else gives it gratis, and either way is awkward. Lyadov charges from six to ten roubles per lesson. Therefore each of us will have to pay anywhere from one to one rouble and seventy kopeks.

Petersburg,
March 30, 1905

...The theory students are sending a statement to the board of directors of the Conservatory saying that since Rimsky-Korsakov, Glazunov and Lyadov have left they no longer want to remain at the conservatory, and asking that their papers be returned to them. They asked me to sign it, and with Mama's permission I did.

You simply can't imagine who is going to replace Rimsky-Korsakov. It turns out that Bernhard, the former director, is going to teach harmony and counterpoint in place of him and Lyadov, whilst Solovyev will be director. It is easy to see why the students are leaving and will take private lessons with Rimsky-Korsakov next year. Many of them say he will teach them free or, if not, will charge ten roubles a lesson.

I went to Winkler's home twice this week. At the last lesson he asked, 'Are you going to stay at the Conservatory?'

'No,' I said, 'I'm leaving.'

'Of course. It's not worthwhile staying on.'

Chernov said the same thing: that Bernhard won't teach anyone anything new.

It turns out that the letter for which Rimsky-Korsakov was dismissed was published in *Russkiye Vedomosti*, No. 2. Please cut it out and save it for me.

PROKOFIEV'S MOTHER TO HIS FATHER:

Petersburg,
March 31, 1905

Our country is now passing through such an unprecedented period that every day brings new things, as though it was a new year. Last autumn we sent our son to the Conservatory, and now in the spring we are taking him back. Could one have imagined that?

We have had to find out, to our cost, that one cannot swim against the current.

All the theory students are leaving and will be going to the office at the same time to get their papers back. Personally, I am convinced that everything will be straightened out, that Rimsky-Korsakov will be director; that the other professors will come back; and that the students will be admitted again. If the worst comes to the worst, Serezha will have to club together with the other students and take private lessons from one of the professors, thus doing the year's work outside the Conservatory.

But what else can be done? When we see you again, we can discuss it together.

PROKOFIEV TO HIS FATHER:

Petersburg,
April 3, 1905

Lyadov said that in all likelihood Rimsky-Korsakov would not come back to the Conservatory. For two years he has been saying that he would leave it: he wants to lead a quieter life and compose. But if the board of directors asks his forgiveness and gives him satisfaction in general, Glazunov and Lyadov will come back to the Conservatory. Glazunov will teach free composition and fugue in addition to orchestration, and Lyadov will teach harmony and counterpoint.

Tomorrow I am taking Winkler the last movement of Beethoven's *Sonata*

No. 7 (it is the eighth sonata I have worked on with him) and [Bach's] *Fugue No. 13*. (This is the thirteenth fugue I have studied with him.)

Nicolas Miaskovsky (1881-1950) was to be one of Prokofiev's closest and oldest friends. He was born in a fortress, the son of a general in the Russian army and actually trained for the army. (He fought from 1914-1916). Like Prokofiev he went to the Conservatory of St Petersburg and studied under Rimsky-Korsakov. After the war he became a professor of composition at the Conservatory of Moscow.

Prokofiev had recently been rather critical of Miaskovsky's compositions.

MIASKOVSKY TO PROKOFIEV AT SONTSOVKA

Oranienbaum,
July 12 1907
Received July 18, 1907

Most Beloved Sergei Sergeyevich

I have been waiting – but in vain, until just now – for an opportunity to respond in worthy fashion both to your letter and (especially, of course) to the puppies you sent me. From the totality of what I have 'created' during this time, I could find nothing that had the slightest chance of pleasing you, so I have decided simply to send you an 'empty' letter without any enclosures – in doing which I am of course showing you the blackest kind of ingratitude. But there it is...

Your music gladdened me to the point of clouding my mind. Along with your repulsive scribbling of the most frightful combinations there are some rather convincing moments. And the over-all tone, the overwhelming ardour, and that causticity which I am so extremely fond of in you, if one may so express it, are so vivid that they unquestionably make up for their defects. At the outset I was of course annoyed that I could play only one note with each hand, and at the opposite ends of the keyboard at that. But when I played the pieces at a tempo (half as fast as yours, of course) that enabled me to understand the general tone, I was fully satisfied – especially with the first piece. The second has more mud in it and is somehow more vulnerable.

So far as the title of the second piece is concerned, I have nothing to say. In general I am not fond of titles, and so I immediately liked the second piece as it was, without any name. *Carnival* is fitting for the first piece: it has a lot of recklessness in it. Perhaps some carnival character would be suitable for the second piece, too: its beginning reminds me of Mime and his sobbing. Incidentally, my opinion is that the last *piu mosso* in the first piece would be improved if you wrote it as follows: octaves in the left hand instead of the four quavers, semi-quavers in the right hand to correspond to the broken chords, and the tempo left unchanged. The way you have written it, one doesn't immediately grasp the change in tempo; since your indications do not explain that the actual speed is doubled. I concluded from the notations on the 'things' that they were my property, and hence I shall not return them. If, of course, you do not agree with my conclusion, I shall proceed as you direct me by letter.

All my plans for orchestral diversions have foundered on my profound laziness and sluggishness. I can't get beyond the confines of the piano – and occasionally piano and voice. I constantly muddle along with such trifles as my *Third Piano Sonata* (in two movements, the first being a small three-voice fugue, *Lento*). Also out of sheer idleness I have thrown together a dozen fragments for piano; some of which are indecently brief (eight bars): and risky. I really can't bring myself to send them along. Last week I set seven poems by Baratinsky to music, but the songs are very ordinary and would be of no interest to you.

One of my most piquant amusements this summer has been the study of harmony with Monsieur Kobylyansky, whom Lyadov sent me – no doubt in order to exasperate me completely. Every Tuesday he comes to fish out fifths and octaves, play totally nonsensical modulations, and in between listen to heartrending love songs and frivolous things from operettas. There's pleasure for you! In a few days I'm going to Asafyev's to recover. I'll be expecting your sonata and sonatina.

Goodbye for now,

Yours,
N. Miaskovsky

MIASKOVSKY TO PROKOFIEV

Sontsovka,
15 September 1908

Dear Nikolay Yakovlevich:

Today I completed my symphony. It came out to 131 pages (57+19+55), with enough music for twenty-eight minutes; that is a bit longer than I wanted.

Because of the cholera we shall be a bit late in getting to Petersburg. We are afraid of it, but will set out as soon as it slackens off.

Did you finish your symphony: If not, finish it. If so, don't show it to anyone – wait for me. And *don't so much as mention it to Liadov*, because there's no sense in showing it to him. Glazunov may arrange a performance for us. But Liadov?...He'll just revile us.

Prokofiev was deeply affected by Stravinsky's music, especially his works written for Diaghilev's Ballet Russe. He was to see performances of *The Nightingale*, *The Firebird* and *Petrushka* whilst visiting Europe in 1913. They formed an uneasy friendship but Prokofiev was often jealous.

On 4 August 1925 Prokofiev writes to Miaskovsky saying:

'Stravinsky has written a dreadful sonata, which he plays himself with a certain chic. The music is Bach but with pockmarks.'

In 1928 he referred to Stravinsky's *Apollo* as 'a terrible bore'.

However, they remained friends, enjoying swapping stories and sharing a mutual love of Europe.

PROKOFIEV TO STRAVINSKY

18 rue Troyon, Paris XVII
29 Nov. 1926

Dear Igor Fyodorovich,

Please be so kind as to tell me the address of the company that taught you how to drive an automobile. As it happens we have taken up residence in the neighbourhood and would like to make use of the proximity.

Cordial greetings from us both.

Your
S Prkfv

The death of Miaskovsky in 1950 was a great sadness to Prokofiev. The following are their last letters.

23 April 1950
Dear Serrozhechka, congratulations on your 59th birthday! I embrace you heartily and hope to see you at Nikolina Gora in the best of health.

Forgive me for the parcel, it might not suit your taste; but for some reason I took a fancy to it at once. We were all delighted with your *Bonfire*.

Warm regards to Mira Alexandrovna.

With all my heart

N. Miaskovsky

Enraptured with Cinderella!

Prokofiev's reply:

16 May 1950

Dear Nikolay Yakovlevich,

I embrace you with all my heart. I think of you all the time. Come to Nikolina Gora as soon as possible.

Your

S.P.

IVOR GURNEY

1890–1937

Ivor Gurney was a poet and composer. During the First World War he served on the Western Front and was wounded and gassed. After the war he became increasingly unsettled and was committed to a mental institution in 1922, spending the rest of his life in care. He continued to write poetry. He was a great friend of Herbert Howells (1892–1990) who was a composer of church music and who succeeded Holst as Director of Music at St Paul's Girls' School.

IVOR GURNEY TO HERBERT HOWELLS

? Feb 1917

My Dear Howler,

It is too bloody cold to write in this barn, but you having been sick and polite to my 'Flanders' barge, deserve a note longer than this will be.

I hope old chap your health is not more shaky than the weather might excuse; our promising young genius must not fade away as a flower; we have not enough seeds.

And thanks for playing commercial traveller to me. By the way has Allen seen your Concerto? Very much I wish to hear that again, being bon and far from na pooh finis encore.

Here the country is fine and marked with 1870 earthworks. A huge rock towers out above the town which being interpreted is the star. Quite a revela-tion of beauty after grey desolations.

What stunt are you on now? I wait for the Violin Sonata clear fairly simple with the romantic slow movements singing of Western things. Show us Tintern and sunset across the Malvern and Welsh Hills. Make us see the one evening star among the trees. And the Scherzo of this String Quartet- a great Spring Wind blowing the hair of the exultant traveller wandering without purpose save to find beauty and to be comrade with the wind.

O to be back with you ...

Well what is Germany's game now? What will come of the clash of the Tirpitz and Bethmann Hollweg parties?

General January has fought for us, though a hard master he was, but le General Fevrier is even more terrible.

I want you to see a thing just sent by me to Miss Scott, called either 'Beauty' or 'Winter Beauty'. In this two lines you will like.

'Yet O, the star-born passion of Beethoven,
Makes consolation on the quivering strings'.
Pencil bust. Time to finish.
Good luck,
Plenty tuck,
Tunes in the noddle
For Concert-stück

Yours ever
IVOR GURNEY

choral & orchestral work; the singing of the children especially was a revelation.

In all the advanced classes there was displayed a quite uncommon appreciation of the poetical possibilities of the music, & the words were pronounced and (apparently) understood by the singers in a refreshingly sure way. Soon – a good day for art when it arrives – we shall all know the difference between sentiment and romance, and between what is theatrical & what is dramatic: these distinctions are unknown to many critics and to more performers – all of whom might have listened to a considerable portion of the Morecambe Festival with advantage.

I cannot well express what I feel as to the immense influence your Festival must exert in spreading the love of music; it is rather a shock to find Brahms's part-songs appreciated & among the daily fare of a district apparently unknown to the sleepy London Press; people who talk of the spread of music in England & the increasing love of it rarely seem to know where the growth of the art is really strong and properly fostered. Some day the Press will awake to the fact, already known abroad and to some few of us in England, that the living centre of music in Great Britain is not London, but somewhere farther North.

... In conclusion I will say it was a unique pleasure to hear so much that was truly admirable, & I look forward to the next Morecambe Festival with keen pleasure; I think it amply worth a long journey to be a listener, and as the enthusiasm is somewhat unusual to the eyes of a chorally-starved southerner, may I say a spectator also?

I offer you a personal congratulation on the great organization you have called into being, & trust you may long be able to direct & advise your coadjutors.

Believe me,
Yours sincerely,
Edward Elgar.

Troyte Griffith was a very old friend. He was an architect and very witty. In his later years Elgar seemed to have no hesitation in asking him to do all manner of odd jobs and in the following letter Elgar writes to him shortly after his investiture with the Order of Merit at Buckingham Palace. His gratification and pride are evident – and he has a small errand for Troyte.

ELGAR TO TROYTE GRIFFITH

Royal Societies Club
St James's Street,
S.W
July 11, 1911

My dear Troyte,

They have made me a life member of the club! dependant on the O.M.

I hope to see you soon as our tenure of the house in Gloucester Place expires next Saty. week.

I wish you wd. write to the Worcester paper & say a little what the Order of M really is! Some of the (locals?) think it is a sort of degradation & quite unworthy of me. I see in the festival* list of (Honours?) they have put it *after* Mus. D. etc. At the investiture Sir A. Trevelyan & I were marshalled next G.C.B. & *before* G.C.M.G. (which is Ld. Beauchamp's highest distinction!) & of course before G.C.S.I. etc. It was very nice.

My portrait is done; it is part of the plan, a rule laid down by Kg. Edward that all members of the order shd. have their portraits "drawn" at the King's expense & hang in Windsor Castle! There.

I wish you cd. come up & see Kelston before the workmen wade in. Is there a Lodging near you vacant for a day or two next week? Write to A. please.

Ever yrs.
Ed. Elgar

On August 4th 1914 war broke out and a feeling of patriotism swept through the country. The first Promenade Concert of the season took place at Queen's Hall on Saturday August 15th. It was an emotional evening, *Land of Hope and Glory* taking pride of place.

Elgar was determined to do his bit for the war effort. He joined the Special Constabulary and was soon promoted to the position of Staff Inspector.

In this impassioned letter to his old friend and wealthy patron of the arts, Frank Schuster, Elgar describes London at the outbreak of the war and reveals his passion for horses.

* *Worcester*

sometimes, I conclude that 'tis want of ability and get in a mouldy desponding state which is really horrible.'

In May 1889 Elgar married Alice Roberts, a wealthy woman in her mid-thirties, who resolved to make Edward into a great composer.

In 1900 Elgar finished *The Dream of Gerontius* set to the poem by Cardinal Newman.

ELGAR TO NICHOLAS KILBURN (FRIEND AND AN AMATEUR MUSICIAN)

29th June 1900
Craeg Lea
Wells Road
Malvern

My dear Kilburn

I am so very glad you have broken silence – I wondered if I'd done any-thing wrong!

Now: your letter is good to have but echoes some sadness – this is not my practical concern but I must send a line to say how I feel very deeply in a friend's – is it? – trouble.

I hope all is over and past that has been disagreeable. No more. My work is good to me and I think you will find Gerontius far beyond anything I've yet done – I *like* it – I am not suggesting that I have risen to the heights of the poem for one moment – but on our hillside night after night looking across 'Mimitable' horizon (Pleonasm!) I've seen in thought, the Soul go up and have written my own heart's blood into the score.

You must hear it at Birmingham.

You asked me this or I wd not have talked about myself or doings.

Deo Gratias: we are all well and flourishing after influenza and much love from us all to you all.

Yours ever
Ed: Elgar

To Nicholas Kilburn
Craeg Lea
Malvern
June (1902) 7.02

My dear Kilburn

We only reached home last night after our long German rambles: we had a complete rest and no letters forwarded – I fear you have been thinking evil things of me (don't) on acct. of my silence. 'High Tide' is impossible now, as I am, when permitted, engaged on mightier stuff. I should have delighted in assisting in your Middlesborough fest but I cannot permit a new work.

We had a glorious time at Dusseldorf. Strauss' speech has been misunderstood (deliberately?) by the village organist type in England.

Thanks for all you say.

My wife is tired and is resting in bed, but joins me in much love to you all.

Yours ever
Edward Elgar

Strauss is absolutely great – wonderful and terrifying, but somewhat cynical – his music I mean. *He* is a real clever good man.

> During the next few years Elgar produced *The Apostles*, The *Cockaigne Overture* and the second of the *Pomp and Circumstance Marches*, *The Coronation Ode*, which was to give us *Land of Hope and Glory*, and *Dream Children*.
>
> By now Elgar was a well-known personality. However, his occasional pomposity and pride and in this instance, his extreme honesty, cannot have endeared him to his London critics. He wrote the following letter to Canon Gorton at the conclusion of the Morecambe Festival of 1903 and it was published in the Musical Times for July.

ELGAR TO CANON GORTON

Dear Canon Gorton,

I should like to thank you and the Committee for the pleasant time I spent at the Morecambe Festival.

I was delighted, & will add surprised, at the general excellence of the

ARTHUR BLISS
1891–1975

Arthur Bliss was born in London and studied first at Cambridge and then under Vaughan Williams and Stanford at the Royal College of Music. Apart from his work on compositions, Bliss was Musical Director of the BBC from 1941-1944 and in 1953 became Master of the Queen's Musick.

ARTHUR BLISS TO THE PALL MALL GAZETTE
Published in the issue dated 11 October 1916

Sir,

As one of those musicians who have fought German aggression in France, I should like to express my thanks to Edwin Evans and 'Musicus' for their championship of English music and their fight against the predominating influence of Germany at home.

It seems to me unseemly that a fine institution like the London Symphony Orchestra should have to put its financial security in front of its national feelings – if all had followed suit we should never have declared war. Moreover, by its choice of works it has missed a signal opportunity of showing its appreciation and gratitude to those of the profession who are fighting to maintain all the cherished institutions of this country.

The names of two such occur instantly to my mind. One is Dr. R. Vaughan Williams, who for eighteen months had been through the drudgery of a private's work in the R.A.M.C., the other is Lieutenant G.S.K. Butterworth, M.C. who was killed in action. The works of either would add to the prestige of the English orchestra that included them in its programme; nor do I think that a performance of Vaughan William's Symphony in London would be altogether unfitting at this time. I am delighted to think that Dr. Allen is doing the 'Sea Symphony', together with works by Stanford and Parry later in the season to commemorate those of the Senior Service who have died. All honour and success to him!

I do not know whether as a class musicians have been less affected (except financially) than other professions, but when straight from being wounded on the Somme I went into a London concert hall and heard a public vociferously applauding a German soloist, it gives me furiously to think.

FRANCIS POULENC
1899–1963

Poulenc was born in Paris and before he became a composer he was a pianist studying with Ricardo Vines to whom he said that he owed everything. Even after attaining maturity as a composer he is still remembered as a pianist, and in particular for his celebrated partnership with Pierre Bernac and performances of Satie's music. Many of his most important scores are for the piano. He was a loyal disciple of Satie and a member of the group called 'The Six', which included Durey, Honegger, Milhaud, Germaine Tailleferre and Auric. He was opposed to 'romanticism' and preoccupied most of all with music for wind and voice. He worked closely with his friend Cocteau, the poet, and was associated with Diaghilev and the Ballet Russe, writing ballet scores as well as orchestral works, chamber music, much piano music and some opera and religious works.

FRANCIS POULENC TO RICARDO VINES

26 September 1917

Very urgent

Mon bien cher Maître,

Today I had such a lamentable and stupid experience that I am going to describe it to you and ask for your advice.

Recommended by a friend of mine who is himself on very friendly terms with Paul Vidal*, I went to see the latter to talk to him about the possibility of my entering the Conservatoire.

At the beginning of the visit he was pleasant enough, asking who had been my teachers up to now, and so on. Then he asked if I had brought him a manuscript. I handed him the manuscript of my *Rapsodie nègre*. He read it carefully, wrinkled his brow and, on seeing the dedication to Erik Satie, rolled his eyes in fury, rose and yelled these exact words:

'Your work stinks, it is ludicrous, it is nothing but a load of BALLS. Are you trying to make a fool of me with these consecutive fifths everywhere? And what the hell is this Honoloulou? Ah! I see you have joined the gang of Stravinsky, Satie & Co. well then, I'll say goodbye!' And he almost threw me out. So here I am, high and dry, not knowing what to do or whom to consult.

Could you not give me a letter of recommendation to Ravel or Gédalge?

Paul Vidal was a French conductor, mainly of ballets and operettas. He was also a composer.

They might perhaps help to set me on the right track. Otherwise, well, I suppose I will go to the Schola. But all the same, what a rude man that Vidal is! You should have seen how he spoke of those perpetrators of wrong notes–meaning Srav., Satie, etc. It was enough to make you die with laughter.

I dare to hope, *bien cher Maître*, that despite the many calls on your time you will be good enough to suggest what steps I should take, or else give me a recommendation to Gédalge. I send you my sincere thanks in anticipation.

This business has, I assure you, so much upset my plans that I really need you and your advice.

With kindest regards,
Francis Poulenc
When will you be back in Paris?

FRANCIS POULENC TO JEAN COCTEAU

Chez Madame Berthier,
lingère,
Point-sur-Seine (Aube),
[12 February 1919]

Bon Jean, a fantastic scheme – send me *urgently* a letter, signed Russels, Rally, anything you like provided it sounds American.

In it, say that you have just returned from London and that you want to see me about the edition of my *Rapsodie*, etc...etc...I leave it to your imagination.

With the help of this fake letter I shall try to get leave – in fact, I am sure I will get leave. So write *immediately* and don't give me away to the police.

I am working hard. 'Toréador' for voice and instruments. We can run through it on Saturday if I get leave, so write that letter quickly.

I am counting on you.
Your devoted Francis

In the following letter to Diaghilev, Poulenc demonstrates the number of artists and dancers that he knew in Paris. Otto Marius Kling was the director of the English music publishers (J & W Chester), Jean Aubry was a French writer on music and a promoter, Madame Edwards, a patron of the arts whose salons were frequented by the painters, Toulouse Lautrec, Vuillard and Bonnard, and Massine who was a Russian born dancer and choreographer.

FRANCIS POULENC TO SERGE DIAGHILEV

76 rue de Monceau,
Paris,
Monday, 28 April 1919

Cher Monsieur et Ami,

Thanks to Picasso I have your address at last and am now able to thank you from the bottom of my heart for all you have done for me.

Everything has been agreed between Mr Kling and myself. What is more, he has written me a most charming letter, and in his prompt reply I sense the effect of your warm recommendations. This is why I really do want to express to you all my gratitude.

I had the pleasure of hearing through Jean Aubry that my *Rapsodie* is to be played in London. I am extremely glad to think that you will at last be able to hear it, as the piano version does not really do it justice.

I very often think of the conversation we had at Madame Edwards'. How right you are to ban literature from all choreographic works. Experience proves this only too well, even when one is dealing with great poets. Only the other day Braque said to me: 'Isn't it already a great deal to have to take three people into account, namely the choreographer, the painter and the musician; if you have to include a writer as well, then all unity is sacrificed.' Quite so...

It is really up to the choreographer to work out the scenario and that is why – if it does not put him out and provided he has the time – I should like to correspond with Monsieur Massine to see what we could do.

I hope to hear from you both fairly soon, and send you my respectful compliments. Thank you once again.

Your very devoted
Francis Poulenc

83 rue de Monceau,
Paris,
29 January 1923

Cher Falla,

Yesterday I practically brought the house down with my applause for your *Amour sorcier* which I ADORE. Could you possibly ask Chester to send me the score – I would be so thrilled to have it. Did I ever thank you for your *Fantasie* for the piano? It is an exquisite work. I have scrapped the *Caprice espagnol* – it would not have been worthy of you. I shall dedicate another composition to you, something that I am entirely happy with. I send you a thousand warm regards.

Francis Poulenc

MANUEL DE FALLA TO FRANCIS POULENC

Granada,
5 January 1932

Très cher Poulenc,

My best wishes for a happy New Year and a great thank-you for the joy you have brought by sending me the score of *Aubade* and of the *Concert champêtre*, which now more than ever I long to hear.

Aubade is well suited to the instrumental possibilities of the chamber orchestra of Seville (Orquesta Betica), and I have warmly recommended it to them. Their only fear is of the financial difficulties in hiring the parts, as the orchestra has extremely limited means. I would ask you to kindly warn the publishers of this...

FRANCIS POULENC TO YVONNE GOUVERNE, CHORUS MASTER AND COACH

Monday [1938]

Ma petite Yvonne,

I wish I could express what happiness your all too short visit gave me. Do not thank me for my friendship; if only you knew how *essential* yours is to me. I am afraid, *ma petite Yvonne*, that I turn to you far too often.

Gradually (I am in no hurry) I would like it to be said in Paris that my

Mass is worth working on – with a little bit of faith in the composition itself and a great deal of faith in me. I think Vallombrosa – who wrote me a charming letter – will perhaps be able to arrange something at Saint-Eustache with you. In his letter, his intention was to speak to you about it.

I am also counting on you for a revival of *Sécheresses* next winter with Munch. My first choice of hall would be the Salle Gaveau, perfect in size for this composition. I have just finished amending, revising and polishing it.

My conscience obliges me to say that I was partly at fault. In the first place, for having given in to James by including additional bars for the orchestra between the final cry, *'hear me'* and the conclusion. The only technical thing of which I am more or less *certain* is my sense of prosody. Adding *artificial* bars between an imperative phrase and an explanation is as if a man, ranting and railing, were to yell *'listen to me'*, then go into the room next door and emerge ten minutes later to explain himself. What I would never have conceded to Eluard or to Apollinare – oh! irony – I conceded to James... because he paid me for the work. I wanted him to be happy. You saw the result.

I have also touched up the conclusion very considerably – both in the orchestral part and the choral part. I had dreamed of an unaccompanied choir simply *highlighted* by instrumental touches but I have come to understand that what this created was a watercolour effect in the corner of a painting done in oils.

I confess to feeling very bitter that at my age I am still prone to such errors of 'auditory vision'.

How hard it is to acquire skills when one is still trying to find one's way. I keep seeing this in terms of a ladder, straight and difficult to climb. May God grant me a few more years of health, wisdom and application, so that I may try to leave behind me a little more than the little I have achieved so far.

Believe me, the hours of doubt are dreadful, and the greatness of those I admire – Debussy, Ravel, Strauss, Stravinsky, Falla – must not be obscured by the mediocrity that generally prevails.

I am working feverishly on the Organ Concerto. Two or three songs for Pierre [Bernac] are coming along quickly and well. These flowers make me hopeful of truly beautiful fruits to come. Dear Yvonne, it is very pleasant indeed to be able to say exactly what one thinks about oneself. Believe me, I suffer neither from false modesty, nor from pride, nor from an inferiority complex. I simply try to see things clearly – that is all.

Whereupon I embrace you and send you these songs, more amusing I hope than my prose.

Very fondly,

Francis

Rose Dercourt-Plaut became a devoted friend and correspondent of Francis Poulenc. She was a Polish-American soprano whom he met during his first tour of America, from 1948 – 1949. Poulenc had a weakness for American clothes and often asked Rose to do little shopping errands for him. Fred is Rose's husband.

FRANCIS POULENC TO ROSE DERCOURT-PLAUT

[Brive, Corrèze],

16 June [1956]

Chère petite Rose,

Excuse my dreadful silence but I have had an insane amount of work to do recently. I have just finished the orchestration of *Les Carmélites*. It will be produced in February at La Scala and in March in Paris. I have corrected the piano score, and prepared the concert and lecture that I am giving in Aldeburgh (at the Britten Festival on 24 June). Now that the main work is over I am going to turn my mind to various other things, and primarily to your song [*Nuage*], for which I have already found two bars!!!

Here are my plans: from 26 June to 12 July – Evian. From 12 to 20 – Milan. From 20 to 23 – Aix. From 24 to 28 – American Conservatory in Fontainebleau, where I am giving a course with Bernac on my music. From 28 July to 14 August – Normandy, at my sister's. Then Noizay.

Couldn't you come to Fontainebleau from the 24th, before Enghien? Or could you make a weekend at my sister's in August (two hours away from Paris)? I am of course *counting* on a weekend in September at Noizay with my beloved photographer. I shall not be going to America this winter but certainly next winter. This winter I have my opera everywhere – Milan, Paris, Vienna.

Will you be an angel and slip into your luggage four pairs of socks for me, in nylon without elastic at the calf, two blue and two brown. (I take size 42 in France.) A record of *Les Mamelles* and a cheque book which dear Paffrotti at Salabert's will give you for me. Naturally I will pay you back for the socks and record. What joy to see you again soon. I am marvellously well and am sleeping again without taking anything. Everything is fine with the Destouches. Brigitte [Manceaux] too. We cannot wait to see you. Do, do come to Fontainebleau.

I embrace both you and Fred.

Your devoted
Francis

Will Fred ask Goddard [Lieberson] for the Symphony in C by Igor. Many thanks.

FRANCIS POULENC TO BENJAMIN BRITTEN

Hôtel Splendide,
Evian,
4 July [1956]

Cher Ben,

I want to tell you once again what joy it gave me to be with you at your exquisite Aldeburgh Festival. It was all so much you – full of intelligence, finesse and heart. And from your window, I 'saw' *Peter Grimes*; and in London, I bought the fascinating records of *The Turn of the Screw*. All this has drawn me even closer to you, for whom I have so much love and admiration. Thank you.

The other day I heard an air by Purcell that moved me to tears. It is a passacaglia sung by an alto voice. The continuo on the cello goes something like this:

If you recognise it, can you tell me exactly what it is so that I can buy it. I embrace you, and Peter too.

Francis

13 June [1958],
Feast of St Anthony of Padua!

Mon cher Ben,

By an odd stroke of fortune, your premiere, like that of my *Stabat* in '51, is taking place on the day of the Feast of St Anthony, my favourite saint. May he not take offence at the 'Balloon-breasts' of Therese-Tiresias! I think of you constantly with *wild* regret. I am much better (I am sleeping a little again) but my doctor has once more forbidden me to go near the sea. The long stay in Touraine has done me good. I finished *La Voix humaine* there, a mono-opera by Jean Cocteau.

Do not forget to send me photos. I want to see Peter in a dress. I am sure that, thanks to you, dear Ben, the music will be marvellous.

I was looking forward to this performance so much, and I want to thank you with all my heart for holding it all together and for having so kindly understood that my defection was as melancholy as it was involuntary.

I embrace you as well as Peter.

Your faithful
Francis

Kindest regards to all our friends and especially to the Harewoods.

FRANCIS POULENC TO PIERRE BERNAC

Sheraton Plaza Hotel,
Boston,
Massachusetts,
Tuesday [January 1961]

Mon petit Pierre,

My first long letter is for you. Phone it through to Brigitte afterwards and she will do the same for you with the next letter. The concert here promises to be *very good* . An excellent 'Monique', young, pleasant, catches on quickly and loves my Concerto. As for the *Gloria*, if I had not come here, what peculiar music would have been heard!...

Arriving late for the first rehearsal of the choir, I heard something so unlike me that my legs almost failed me on the staircase. *Excellent* choir but Patterson is not the intuitive Shaw and all those worthy Protestants were singing sharp and shrill (especially the women) as they do in London, with that 'Oh! my good Lord' quality. *All* Munch's tempi were *wrong* – all too fast, naturally. A well-intentioned lady was singing the part of Addison (who had not yet arrived), with a voice like a goat and all out of tune. A pale, wan pianist tinkled the keys, and not always the right ones!! I tell you, I wanted to run a mile. My poor child was really presenting itself badly. What a burden music is!!!...

MSTISLAV ROSTROPOVICH TO FRANCIS POULENC

Mstislav Rostropovitch,
Conservatoire,
Moscow, USSR,
[1961?]

Cher Maitre Monsieur Francis Poulenc!

I beg your pardon for disturbing you with this letter which my friend will deliver to you. For a long time I have been trying to play the cello well, but to tell the truth I do not know if I have succeeded. I have asked my friend to give my letter to you and also the records of the Symphony-concerto by Prokofiev and the one by Shostakovich, which have been dedicated to me. I hope very much that you will listen to them if you have a free moment. I am writing to you because I am one of the great admirers of your music. In autumn, in Edinburgh, I heard your *La Voix Humaine*. It is marvellous...

In all musical literature there is no composition as admirable as the *Poème* for violin by Chausson. But this genre is just as beautiful for the cello, which is able to sing with a 'human voice'. You are the only one who can make it sing as wonderfully as Denise Duval. I beg of you on behalf of cellists the world over to offer this gift to all musicians. Tomorrow I shall be leaving for Mexico and South America. I shall spend a day in London to play with the composer Benjamin Britten, who has dedicated a work to me.

I hope to hear from you. I can think of nothing but this work. If you do write this sonata of my dreams I shall, if you wish, come to Paris for the first performance, then to Moscow, anywhere you like. In Moscow you would be welcomed by all musicians.

Tous mes respects affectueux
et mon amour pour vous
Mstislav Rostropovitch

WILLIAM WALTON
1902–1983

William Walton was born in Oldham. He became a boy chorister at Christ Church Cathedral, Oxford. Later at Oxford University he became involved with Sacheverell Sitwell and through him met his brother Osbert and sister Edith. He wrote the accompanying music for the recitation of Edith's poems, including *Façade*. Later outstanding works included *Sinfonia Concertante* for piano and orchestra, *Portsmouth Point*, *Belshazzar's Feast*, for baritone soloist, chorus and orchestra, the film music for Laurence Olivier's *Henry V* and much more.

Adrian Boult was an orchestral conductor. From 1924 he was in charge of the Birmingham City Orchestra and from 1930, Musical Director of the BBC. In 1950 he became the conductor of the Royal Philharmonic Orchestra in London.

ADRIAN BOULT TO WILLIAM WALTON

13th November, 1932

Many thanks for your letter. I certainly think that we gave a better show of 'Belshazzar' than last time, in particular I think we solved the problem of 'The Kings of the Earth', expensive though the solution is, for as you know the Wireless Chorus is entirely professional. I expect you were able to hear the rather slower tempo and determine whether you found it too slow. Personally I thought it worked out just right though we reduced the Double Basses to two and had a good deal of trouble with the bass line altogether. Bass Clarinet and Bassoons and so on had to be very much damped down. This with rather an exaggeration of the portamento between the high crotchet and quaver of the accompanying figure I think gave the passage its right value and meaning, and the unaccompanied passage finished dead in tune.

One other point; there still seem to be a great many discrepancies between the score and parts in regard to dynamic sounds, in particular a good many of the *ffs* and quiet marks generally in the Feast Scene are missing from the parts. This is very important. It gave us a lot of trouble to scale this time to something that would still leave power in reserve for the final F major.

However, we all enjoyed ourselves very much.

A.C.B.

MICHAEL TIPPETT
1905-

Michael Tippett was born in London and attended the Royal College of Music. He came to the notice of the critics with his *Concerto for Double String Orchestra* (1939) and the oratorio, *A Child of Our Time* (1940). There followed operas, symphonies, sonatas and much chamber work. Benjamin Britten held him in high regard and Tippett in turn respected Britten's genius.

MICHAEL TIPPETT TO ALEC ROBERTSON

Whitegates Cottage
Oxted
Surrey
4 Dec 1942

Dear Alec,

Thanks for your letter of the 27th last. The 31st of Jan is alright, providing I am at large then. I'll keep you informed immediately of anything untoward if it were to happen.

I've been thinking-over lots of ideas, but rather come back to 'Stravinsky & the Dance' or some other such title. I would like to show how deep-seated is his feeling for dance & movement & rhythm – then exemplify his unconscious, perhaps, attitude by playing a few movements from a Bali gong orchestra & then Stravinsky himself a few moments, playing his own Piano Rag music. And so to lead thro [or to] Petrushka & the Russian dance towards some final piece to be played complete: Either a portion of the Symphony of Psalms, or Les Noces (the final scene) – or a [living] 2 pf. version of the Dumbarton Oaks Concerto, 1st movement. The great point about Stravinsky is that the initial musical experience for him, & for his likeness therefore, is abruptly physical & immediate. Played properly it is gay & unsentimental, Exhilarating.

By the way, I'm using the weekend to look at his new Symphony before the score goes to the BBC. Stravinsky's publisher is mine too! All by accident. So what with my natural interest, I have good opportunity to get hold of all I want.

Will you let me know sometime soon if this strikes you as the right idea & then I'd like to get a script out & to you complete as soon as possible.

I had been to supper with Ben & Peter last Saturday. Showed them my magnum opus, an oratorio, called 'A Child of Our Time'. The text is my own, with advice from T S Eliot, & the whole work is modern & contemporary, but religious without being in the cult. Sometime I want to show it to you. Ben has just written me a p.c. 'What a grand work the Oratorio is & A performance *must* be arranged soon.' Easier said than done! But meanwhile Schotts are going to bring out a piano-vocal score as the first move. If you're interested I must try to get hold of a text for you. There were some prints made but I'm short of them. One, by the way, went to Raybould & must be buried in the Corporation [B.B.C.] – wish you could recover it.

I've still no word from Bedford [B.B.C.] as to the Fantasia for Pf & orchestra & a date. But I suppose it'll come one day.

The new Stravinsky score has the same dedication as the Psalm Symphony "Composée à la gloire de Dieu & dediée au Boston Symphony Orchestra". Is he a crozant?

Excuse the rigmarole. I'm feeling v gay as I've finished the new 4tet & it looks like a performance at Wigmore in Feb.

Please let me have a word on the Stravinsky thing – & shall I try my hand at a script?

Yours

The Stravinsky programme was broadcast on 31 January 1943. *A Child of Our Time* received its first performance at the Adelphi Theatre on 19 March 1944; the soloists included Joan Cross and Peter Pears. It was first broadcast on 28 February 1944 in a concert in aid of the children of Poland at the Royal Albert Hall.

In 1943 Tippett was imprisoned for three months for failing to comply with the conditions of his registration as a Conscientious Objector.

MICHAEL TIPPETT TO EVELYN MAUDE

5/7
Number 5834 Name M Tippett
H.M. PRISON WORMWOOD SCRUBS, W.12

Evelyn dear,

Yr letter was a great pleasure to get. I will reply to its contents first. Books – I got the 2 Devotional books, but haven't yet read them. In fact I read little. Cell task occupies a lot of time & there is a baby prisoners orchestra here wh I conduct & try to improve – & that takes 2 hours out of possible reading time. It's a sort of light café orchestra, & with instruments of different pitch – in fact throw-outs. But we manage – & hope to get in better music. On Sunday we are to play in chapel, in the middle of a recital by Peter Pears & Ben Britten – all v. amusing. So don't worry to chase after books. But there is a text-book I'd like (I've got the Bach) – will you ring Alec Robertson & ask him from me if he cld spare me a copy of his book: The Problem of Plainsong – on the art of wh he is an authority. If & when you get it, take it Friends House as you did the Bach. I shdn't send it to Cornford just yet.

Tell Mother if you're writing any time, not to wonder at the letters about me to her – I'm sort of a general favourite. As to getting down there, I might manage after the proper holiday on way back from Cornwall if it's to be there – otherwise I think to write the long delayed 1st movement of the old 4tet. & then take another break away, at Exmouth p'raps, & then start the Symphony – wh will be a big thing.

I agree with you completely abt press hoo-ha – no interested party shld write at all.

Holiday – I'm quite as ready to go with David first. The point is anyhow that I come out Sat. 21st Aug. & will make the 4tet. performance at Wigmore the public meeting ground for all & sundry. Rhse choirs etc – then come home & get things together etc Sunday.

The question of my getting something from people like books is difficult. I don't know for instance how much I really get from David – sometimes I'm rather repressed by him. I get a great deal from you – but that is a more subtle business, & in this case must wait till I'm properly home & at work again.

Keep the Hölderlin, Maritain etc, they're for my library & the autumn.

Haven't read any Paul yet. It hasn't worked out quite as I expected. One gets not only fallow but sluggish. We're all the same. You can't manufacture the proper conditions & there's a lot of internal strain – a great deal of dreaming & inner adjustment – & the weeks inside seem monstrously lengthy & disproportionate, so that you fail to realise how easily they pass to those outside or how little one might oneself get done outside.

As far as I know there is nothing against length in letters in. Write on thin paper perhaps. You might send some 18 or 20 stave score – a few sheets – with the Robertson book. I shall probably get permission to use it. But 12 stave will do, if the other is too big.

And now messages, a special one this time to Ben & Miriam, who use after all my home & my own. Tell Miriam to use the tin of sugar in the larder wh Den gave me, for jam. I shall have forgotten the taste by the time I come out. I have already. Is anyone in the cottage yet?

A message of greeting to the choirs p.o. Tolworth (book under T.): hope they're managing. Write if you will to the deputy Tanner & say he must choose music to suit himself & that I shall probably take at least September clear away for my own work – (if not give the choir up altogether). Ask to pay for those times he deputised for wh I signed the register – & generally to try & solve the payments, claims problems of that choir, via the Sec. of the W.E.A. It is done terminally, & so quite soon. p.o. Tooting (under T.) Just send them greetings, either via Tony or the Sec. Will see them again next term of course.

Morley. Give them best wishes for the concert on the 17th, & hope they do well. Will be thinking of them. You can let them know sometime that I shall make my first reappearance on 21st Aug at Wigmore.

Fresca: Give her my love – tell her I'm managing fine – that I came across a typical Irish ABBA tune in Songs of Praise masquerading as English Traditional Melody. If she thinks to come to the 4tet. on the 21st, would like to lunch with her beforehand, & go with.

If this gets you in time ring Peter & Ben, Primrose 5826 & wish Ben well for his Prom on Sat evening – & tell them not to be distressed by the 'orchestra' in Handel's 'Largo' & Bach's Chorale on Sunday. It's for the sake of social progressiveness not to rival their artistry. If they're still at home on the 21st would like to breakfast with them & bath!

John Amis: Not to forget 6 tickets for Tooting choir via Tony for 17th – & to spare send a couple to Wilf Franks, c/o 45 Holmesdale Rd, N.6. To send my love to the two Walters: to Goehr, not to worry abt the 17th, but that he'll probably gain by all the publicity – & good luck to him & To (Walter) Bergmann my love – & could he possibly begin to look at the printed church music of Weelkes for Morley next season. I think 'Absalom, my son', or some such title a v. fine one. To Schotts in general, Cheminant & Steffens my regards & good wishes. John can do all that. As to visit, the order is due on Mon 19th, but it probably won't reach John till 21st or 22nd. It will have 3 names on it: his, Tony's & Britten's (?) – is that O.K? Otherwise we must invent. All the 3 come together – 2.30 at the prison is a good time. You take a no 7 bus from Oxford Circus to the door (1/2 and hour) or Central London to

Wood Lane, 1 1/2d. Trolley Bus a minute or two to Du Cane Avenue & Walk down 2 or 300 yds. Quite quick. Ring the bell & ask to see me & show the order. Shld like to see read to me any press notices etc.

As to the new 4tet. movement (please keep these notes): I think the 2nd subject needs a longish bit (B) & the repeat of A to lead straight to the constricted portion; probably using some of the old material of [?] to reach the same chord before cello up-going cadenza as before – then a possibly contrapuntal development of wh the reprise of the opening themes will form the climax – & a recapitulation as varied as the material allows & leading by the same coda material to the down-going cello cadenza.

So far I've only had this one 'thought' about my music, as above; I don't think its any good trying to make things move when the circumstances forbid any real output or creation. Prison is not a creative experience at any point – except perhaps in human contacts. I dare say it will seem less wasteful when one looks back – p'raps it may be a real holiday mentally. It's difficult inside not to give exaggerated importance to its actual length of days – & to brood on them so that they go slower. In fact I am pretty active & the time passes somehow.

Razor blades we are allowed to change the permitted one each week. I have 4 only in 'properly' if you post some more to me, they'll just be put with the rest & I can either use them or bring them home. I like to keep shaven & as clean as maybe. It's better for one's self-respect. Any blades that fit a Gillette 3 hole type – or slots.

I've experienced a lucky chance with eye exercises that may be helpful afterwards. Its v. hard on the eyes here. Sewing etc. & bad light in the cell & little time to exercise at all. I shall just about manage to keep them no worse than they are.

One has moments of nostalgia, but not too many. I shall come through. It's boring of course. It *is* good to know things happen outside. Much love to all friends & especially to you.

Michael

I dreamed of a green flowering olive tree in spring last night. Good.

DIMITRI SHOSTAKOVICH
1906–1975

Shostakovich was born in St Petersburg and died in Moscow aged sixty-eight. He studied at the conservatory in St Petersburg and then produced a quick succession of symphonies, operas, piano works and film music. Prokofiev was involved in writing film music in the heady years following the revolution. His music for Eisenstein's film *Alexander Nevsky* was well received and in 1939 he rearranged it for concert performance. Shostakovich had mixed feelings about it.

14.1.1941
Leningrad

Dear Sergey Sergeyevich,

...I recently heard Stasevich perform your *Alexander Nevsky*. Despite a whole series of wonderful moments, I didn't like the work as a whole. It seems to me that artistic norms of some sort have been breached in it. There's too much physically loud, illustrative music. It seemed to me in particular that many sections end before they get started. The beginning of the battle and the entire song for low female voice made a powerful impression on me. Unfortunately, I can't say the same thing about the rest of it. Nevertheless, I'll be immensely pleased if the work receives a Stalin Prize.* For despite its shortcoming this work deserves more than many another candidate...

Generously Shostakovich wrote to Prokofiev after the opening performance of the *Seventh Symphony*. Prokofiev himself was not completely happy with it and his health was fading.

12.X.1952.
Moscow

Dear Sergey Sergeyevich,

Warm congratulations on your wonderful new symphony. I listened through it yesterday with great interest and enjoyment from first to last note. The Seventh Symphony has turned out to be a work of lofty accomplishment, profound feeling, and enormous talent. It is a genuinely masterful work. I am

*It did not.

not a music critic, therefore I shall refrain from more detailed comments. I am simply a listener who loves music in general yours in particular. I regret that only the fourth movement by itself was played as an encore. The whole thing should have been played. For that matter, new works ought to be played twice officially, and the third time for an encore. It seems to me that S.A. Samosud performed the Seventh Symphony superbly.

I wish you at least another hundred years to live and create. Listening to such works as your Seventh Symphony makes it much easier and more joyful to live.

I warmly clasp your hand. Greetings to Mira Alexandrovna.

Yours D. Shostakovich

BENJAMIN BRITTEN
1913–1976

Benjamin Britten was born in Lowestoft and died in Aldeburgh aged sixty-three. He began composition at the age of five. Amongst his most well-known compositions are, *Variations on a Theme by Frank Bridge*, the operas, *Peter Grimes*, *The Rape of Lucretia*, *Albert Herring*, *Billy Budd*, *Gloriana*, *The Turn of the Screw*, *Midsummer Night's Dream* and *Death in Venice*. He also wrote the oratorios, *Noyes Fludde*, *St Nicolas* and the *War Requiem* as well as a *Cello concerto*, *Curlew River*, *The Burning Fiery Furnace* and much more. With Peter Pears, the tenor and his beloved partner, he founded the Aldeburgh Festival.

One of the most important things in Britten's life apart from his music was undoubtedly his relationship with Peter Pears. Their companionship was complete in every way. Peter's voice pleased Britten; it was totally individual. It had none of the operatic Italian tenor about it but neither was it an ecclesiastical church voice. Britten wrote many roles with Peter Pears in mind.

Like Auden, the poet, Britten was a pacifist and felt unable to remain in Britain after the outbreak of the war so he went to America.

However, by the end of the year Britten had decided to return to England. He writes to Mrs Elizabeth Sprague Coolidge, the elderly patron of music whose Coolidge Foundation had commissioned a string quartet from him:

18 October 1941

I have made up my mind to return to England, at anyrate for the duration of the war. I am not telling people because it sounds a little heroic, which it is far from being – it is really that I cannot be separated any longer from all my friends and family – going through all they are, and I'm afraid will be, in the future. I shall continue with my work over there, which is what I most want to do, of course. I don't actually know when I shall be sailing, since boats are scarce & heavily booked up – and anyhow I have so much to get finished here, so I may not be leaving much before Christmas.

In 1944 he got down to writing the opera, *Peter Grimes*. He had been inspired to do this after reading, whilst in Los Angeles, *The Borough* by George Crabbe.

BRITTEN TO PETER PEARS

10 January 1944

Well, at last I have broken the spell and got down to work on P.G. I have been at it for two days solidly and got the greater part of the Prologue done. It is *very* difficult to keep that amount of recitative moving, without going round & round in circles, I find – but I think I've managed it. It is also difficult to keep it going fast & yet paint moods & characters a bit. I can't wait to show it to you. Actually in this scene there isn't much for you to do (I haven't got to the love duet yet); it is mostly for Swallow, who is turning out quite an amusing, pompous old thing! I don't know whether I shall ever be a good opera composer, but it's wonderful fun to try once in a way!

The opera, when first performed at Sadlers Wells, was a great success causing much critical acclaim.

In 1951, when he was busy scoring *Billy Budd*, he decided not to see the new Stravinsky opera, *The Rake's Progress*, with libretto by Auden and Chester Kallman. It was to open in Venice. However, he wrote to the Harewoods:

I feel miserably disappointed (I have done since I first saw the libretto & first few pages of the score) that easily the greatest composer alive should have such an irresponsible & perverse view of opera, (of the voice & of the setting of words & of characterisation in particular). Of course I am sure it will contain a lot of beautiful music, & it will be throughout original & distinguished, but I'm not yet convinced that it helps to keep opera alive one little bit – & I feel Auden to be largely to blame, being the cleverer & more sophisticated of the two. What these two *could* have produced – ! But the subject seems quite wrong for them both.

> Whether this highlights the perennial problem of getting the libretto right or whether this is some little personal cattiness, we can only judge by listening to the opera. Auden in turn, on visiting England in 1953, went to see Britten's *Gloriana*. Afterwards he wrote to Elizabeth Mayer (his host whilst in America) that it had "some of the best operatic music in it, I think, that Ben has done yet...Didn't care for the libretto..."
> After the premiere of *Gloriana*, Britten wrote to the librettist, William Plomer:

I expect that you, like me, have felt a bit kicked around over it – perhaps *more than* me, because I'm a bit more used to the jungle! But the savageness of the wild beasts is always a shock.

> Britten wrote to Eric Walter White two months after the premiere of *The Turn of the Screw:*

I am delighted in your reaction to my latest baby – one is always so delighted that one's sympathetic friends find the last work the best. It was certainly a difficult work to bring off technically and spiritually.

> And to Desmond Shawe-Taylor during the same month:

I think in many ways you are right about the subject being, as it were, nearest to me of any I have yet chosen, (although what that indicates of my own character I shouldn't like to say!)

Like many famous composers Britten was in demand for advice and lessons for hopeful young composers. One of the people he corresponded with was the young Robert Saxton to whom he wrote the following:

BRITTEN TO ROBERT SAXTON

If it worries you too much to work away from the piano, I should go back to it. Only try & think what kind of thing you want to write *before* you sit down at it. And remember that there won't always be 10 fingers playing the music – that violins, oboes & voices work differently from pianos... Try & think of the melody, the rhythm, the accompaniment, the colour of it all (what instruments) as far as possible all together! Certainly not always just the tune first. (I am sure that in Schubert's Trout he thought of the accompaniment first.) Go on writing, play & sing as much of what you write as you can, & find out *why* you don't like the bits that don't work.

The love that Britten held for Peter Pears continued and was reciprocated:

BRITTEN TO PETER PEARS

17th November 1974

My darling heart (perhaps an unfortunate phrase – but I can't use any other) I feel I must write a squiggle which I couldn't say on the telephone [to New York] without bursting into those silly tears – I do love you so terribly, not only glorious *you*, but your singing. I've just listened to a re-broadcast of Winter Words (something like Sept. '72) and honestly you are the greatest artist that ever was – every nuance, subtle & never over-done – those great words, so sad & wise, painted for one, that heavenly sound you make, full but always coloured for words & music. What *have* I done to deserve such an artist and *man* to write for? I had to switch off before the folk songs because I couldn't [take] anything after –'how long, how long' [*The last song of the Hardy cycle*]. How long? – only till Dec. 20th – I think I can just bear it.
But I love you,
I love you,
I love you —

B

Briiten's health continued to deteriorate. In 1975 he went on holiday to Venice. It was a poignant trip for he was very weak and by the time he returned to England he was in a wheelchair. It was in Venice that he completed his String Quartet No. 3. Benjamin Britten died on the 4th December, 1976. Peter Pears was with him.

ACKNOWLEDGEMENTS

The Musician's World Letters, ed. Hans Gal, Thames and Hudson, 1965.
From Parry to Britten by Lewis Foreman, B.T. Batsford, 1987.
The New Grove Bach Family by Christopher Wolff, Macmillan.
The Letters of Beethoven, ed. Emily Anderson, Macmillan, 1961.
The Memoirs of Hector Berlioz, ed David Cairns, Panther, 1970.
Benjamin Britten a Biography by Humphrey Carpenter, Faber & Faber, 1992.
Debussy by Edward Lockspeiser, J.M. Dent & Sons, 1980.
Delius: A Life in Letters 1862–1908 by Lionel Carley, London Scolar Press in association
with The Delius Trust, 1983
Dvorak by Alec Robertson, J.M. Dent & Sons, 1964.
Antonin Dvorak: Letters and Reminiscences, translated Roberta Finlayson Samson,
Prague: Artia, 1954.
Dvorak by Hans-Hubert Schönzeler, Marion Boyars Publishers, 1984.
Elgar O.M. by Percy M. Young, White Lion Publishers, 1973.
The Collected Correspondence and Papers of Christoph Willibald Gluck, edited by Hedwig
& E H Mueller Von Ason, Barrie & Rockliff, London
Handel by Christopher Hogwood, Thames and Hudson,
The New Monteverdi Companion, ed. Denis Arnold and Nigel Fortune, Faber and Faber,
1985.
Mozart's Letters, ed. Eric Blom, Penguin Books, 1956.
Francis Poulenc Echo and Source Selected Correspondence 1915-1963, ed. Sidney
Buckland, Victor Gollancz, 1991.
Prokofiev by David Gutman, The Alderman Press, 1988.
Prokofiev by Prokofiev, A Composer's Memoir, Macdonald General Book, Macdonald
and Jane's, London & Sydney, Translation 1979 Doubleday & Co Inc, Garden City,
New York.
Puccini: A Critical Biography by Mosco Cerner.
Satie Seen Through His Letters by Ornella Volta translated by Michael Buelock,1989,
Marion Boyars Publishers Ltd
Schubert a Biography, George R. Marek, Robert Hale, 1985.
Clara Schumann The Artist and the Woman, Nancy B. Reich, Victor Gollancz, 1985
Piotr Ilyich Tchaikovsky Letters to His Familly, translated by Galina von Meck, Stein and
Day, 1982.
Verdi: A Life in The Theatre by C. Osborne, Weidenfeld and Nicolson, 1987.
The Real Wagner by Rudolph Sabor, André Deutsch, 1987.
The translations of the Janacek letters are by Patrick and Jaroslava Lambert.